A Ministry of Presence

Organizing, Training, and Supervising
Lay Pastoral Care Providers in
Liberal Religious Faith Communities

Rev. Denis Meacham, D.Min.

Published by eBookIt.com

ISBN-13: 978-1-4566-2391-3

To all those lay pastoral care providers
with whom I have worked,
from whom I have learned, and whose creativity
and dedication to their ministries
have inspired their congregations and me

Contents

Prologue

What does it mean to grow spiritually? How we behave, learn, and grow religiously will be defined by the wisdom and teachings of our faith tradition. But the spiritual growth of any human being is measured by the same yardstick: progress from self-centeredness to an ever-expansive love and compassionate concern for others. All the major faith traditions express the same fundamental teaching regarding this pattern of personal growth. This teaching is summarized in what we have come to know as the Golden Rule.

As far as we know, the earliest formulation of the Golden Rule as a spiritual and moral precept is attributable to the Chinese philosopher Confucius (551–479 BCE). It was his insight that there can be no harmony among people, either in the family or in the larger society, unless one makes an effort to transcend one's self-interest. Although Confucius lived millennia before human beings would develop a formal study and understanding of the self and the workings of the human ego, his insight suggests the clear sense that our most basic instinct as living creatures is to secure our own needs, even at the expense of the needs of others. But if our actions are always self-serving, we will inevitably hurt others and be hurt in return. Instead, we must seek an expansion of our life focus from the impulse to secure our own well-being to an altruistic commitment to ease the suffering of others, even at the risk of our own comfort, wealth, or safety.

Confucius could be considered the father of the notion of civility, and indeed, his writings focused on how self-interest on the part of civic leaders could endanger the well-being of an entire society. But his understanding embraced not only army generals and political potentates in their dealings with their constituencies but also the behavior of the individual members of a family. If we conduct our lives with consideration for others and with an awareness of how our behavior affects their lives, we are more likely to create justice and harmony in the body politic as well as in the home. To move beyond selfishness we must consider in all circumstances how we would wish to be treated, and then act accordingly toward others. And we must accept that living in harmony with others always requires a measure of self-denial.

In these teachings Confucius stands at the front of a long line of teachers of the moral life. The central message of the Buddha, the commandments (mitzvoth) given in the Torah, the ministry of Jesus, and the revelations of the prophet Muhammad collected in the Koran are identical: Do to others as you would have them do to you (or, in its negative form: Do not do to others what you would not have them do to you). We must live in loving-kindness with all beings and through acts of compassion ease the burden of others.

In modern times there have been exemplars of a life dedicated to the Golden Rule, modeling compassion and loving-kindness not as religious leaders but as civic leaders whose actions bespeak the centrality of the Golden Rule to a moral life no matter what one's faith tradition. Such figures as Gandhi and Martin Luther King Jr. have taught us that whatever attitudes or behaviors we expect to see in others we must first adopt ourselves.

But the call of the Golden Rule may be missed even by those who consider themselves devoutly religious. It is not prayer, meditation, the studying of sacred texts, espousing creeds, or believing in God (or not believing in God) that represents an honoring of the Golden Rule, it is action: "*Do* to others..." Insofar as prayer or creedal beliefs support acts of compassionate care for others, only then do they contribute to our religious or spiritual growth. As liberal religious people of faith, we profess the worth and dignity of every human being and our conviction to support others' search for spiritual wholeness and well-being. We call these convictions our "principles," but until they are translated into action, we have not been faithful to the values our principles embody.

Thus, in the Golden Rule, all the great faith traditions teach the need for self-transcendence through altruistic behavior. Implicit in this teaching is that such transcendence also expands the well-being of the altruistic person. Again in a foreshadowing of our modern understanding of psychology, the Golden Rule intimates that while our more primitive instinct is to serve the self, in organized society there is a higher impulse, indeed the ground of our humanity: To live a life of ever-expansive love toward all beings. It is just this expansiveness that we refer to as spiritual growth.

Our challenge as people of faith is to overcome our personal barriers to empathetic concern and support for our fellow human beings. These barriers can be discovered through introspection. If our hearts are full of anger, resentment, envy, or fear, it is difficult to be concerned about others. Yet simply recognizing such feelings in ourselves tells us much about how those in distress are feeling. In this recognition of the commonality of suffering, we can begin to let go of our distress, let go of our sense that our hurt is unique, and begin to understand in what ways we need to treat others to relieve the pain and suffering that are unavoidable aspects of the human condition. Recognizing this affinity we have with others can allow us to empathize—to feel how they are feeling, to know what it is like to be the victim of debasing, dehumanizing, or other traumatizing life events. By empathizing we move our attention from ourselves to the other. Such empathy can begin to bring us a measure of serenity and strength. Empathy is transformative in its impact on our well-being. Understanding how we respond to the stresses of life is a prescription for our own psychological and spiritual healing. Understanding how we have healed in cases of our woundedness constitutes the prescription for healing those in our care.

A faith community provides an environment that is meant to contribute to our becoming better people, to increase the good in the world, to make the world a place where more people can thrive. By participating in a faith community, we expect the teachings of our faith to inspire growth within ourselves in terms of our most deeply held values and how we interact with our fellow human beings. As pastoral care providers, our churches afford us a context in which we are compassionately supported in our self-examination and in observing our inclinations to self-centeredness. We receive training in how best to be useful to others in need. In supervision, we can learn to see how our own well-being is essential to our usefulness to others. We can ask ourselves what has helped us (or would have helped us) when we have been hurt. The answers to this question can energize our movement toward a path of altruism. When we understand what *we* need, we will know what we can give to others. Our conclusions may be and often are very simple: What has been important to us in times of distress was the kindness, the compassionate presence of another, the promise that we would not have to endure our travails alone. As we shall see below, the greatest gift we typically can give to another in troubled times is our empathic concern and the promise of companionship through the dark hours. With the support, understanding, insight, and experience of our colleagues and our supervisor, we can come to discern the obstacles in ourselves to becoming effective in our ministries of compassionate care. It is exactly in the formal organization of a lay pastoral care provider program that a safe place is created for us to do our work of introspection and self-care, preparing us to move into the world as healers.

Certainly it is possible to experience spiritual growth outside a faith community, with other than religious influences or teachings to motivate and sustain us. But the opportunity to participate in the good works of our faith community is a gift we should take very seriously. Our conviction that the Golden Rule is fundamental to our humanity and a commitment to its realization through empathic, compassionate acts of kindness to others are the gifts offered to us who respond to the call to a ministry as lay pastoral care providers.

Introduction

In one form or another, it is an oft-repeated scenario: A congregant suffers the loss of a loved one and receives quick and heartfelt attention from the minister and fellow church members. Soon, however, the congregant is left to a very private and often prolonged grief as the pastor and other church members return to the routines of their lives and the attention demanded by the challenges of daily living. Parishioners can fall off the church community's radar screen, sometimes in pain or distress, and when their church doesn't maintain contact with them, they may feel compelled to look elsewhere for spiritual healing. Parish ministers are expected to respond to the spiritual needs of each and every parishioner, but, overburdened by other duties and often with little specialized training, they can find themselves in a losing battle.

Three historically unique developments have put enormous pressure on ministers and congregants to maintain pastoral care services beyond the usual short period that constitutes a crisis in a person's life. First, we live in a time when members of an extended family can no longer be counted on to remain in close proximity. In past generations, people confronting difficult life circumstances could rely on family to provide the support they needed. Today, far-flung vocational opportunities lure people away from their childhood homes to settle not just down the road but across the state or country. Meanwhile, Mom and Pop are moving through the time of life when they are likely to need ongoing attention and care.

Second, we now live with an increasingly aging population. According to the Department of Health and Human Services, approximately 9 percent of adults were over the age of sixty-five in the year 2000; by 2030, that number will rise to more than 20 percent—one in five adults will be a senior citizen. A social science pundit has predicted that it will not be long before we have more adults in day care than children. This trend will have a considerable impact on all aspects of society, none more so than our faith communities. How we have traditionally organized our church lives—governance, mission, polity, and programming—will become less relevant to an ever-increasing number of our congregants. There will be more and more seniors in our congregations whose quality of life, at least in part, will depend on the availability of long-term attention and support from their church community. The active elderly will contribute in new ways and bring new spiritual insight to our church lives, while the frail elderly will require more pastoral care. In my hospice work I have seen the unraveling of families trying—often from a distance—to care for slowly declining loved ones. These elderly loved ones, easily confused and unprepared for the novelty of our fast-paced, technology-driven lifestyles, are especially vulnerable to the complexities of our fractured health care system. If our church communities did nothing but review the current needs of these folks and organize to respond to them, we could substantially improve their lives, especially as community health and social services fall victim to local, state, and federal budget cuts.

The third development is in part responsible for our aging population: People no longer die in great numbers as they once did from acute illness. Through the nineteenth century the leading causes of death were infectious diseases such as tuberculosis, pneumonia, influenza, and syphilis. Today, most folks decline slowly with chronic wasting illnesses. According to U.S. Center for Health statistics, the top killers are heart disease, cancer, stroke, respiratory illnesses, and Alzheimer's. The medical, social, and pastoral care needs of church members with such illnesses may go on for decades. But it doesn't have to be a special population that calls us to a more vigorous pastoral care effort in our faith communities. Any one of us may need compassionate attention from someone willing to be present to us as we move through a time of trial and distress.

Parish ministers, even in small churches, cannot keep up with all the pastoral care needs of their congregations. Even if they have the time, their training in this area may not give them an easy confidence in providing pastoral care. I have learned through personal experience that a well-organized, trained, and supervised cadre of lay ministers can ensure that no member of a congregation of any size ever falls through the cracks. This is the hopeful conviction that has prompted me to write this book.

The provision of pastoral care by lay volunteers is one activity among many that falls within the broader category of lay ministry. I will have more to say about this distinction below. Meanwhile, as I have gone around the country doing workshops on lay pastoral care, I've encountered many versions of lay ministry in general and lay pastoral care specifically—programs that differed in organization, goals, training, supervision, and effectiveness. In some churches, disparate lay ministry programs operate independently of one another. Such separation represents a lost opportunity to integrate resources, training and supervision, needs assessment, and cross communication concerning pastoral care in the church. In another scenario, there is a small lay ministry team trying to do it all, with lay volunteers bravely calling upon a hodgepodge of competencies to carry out their pastoral care mission in the congregation. It is my experience that many lay pastoral care programs, while well intended, function nowhere near the level that would prove useful to all the congregants and allow the parish minister to feel confident that everyone who needs attention and care is receiving it. My travels have encouraged me to present an expanded model of lay pastoral care that can be adapted by any religious community to create a well-organized and successful program.

This new vision of lay pastoral care is an ambitious one, both in terms of the expectations it places on its volunteer participants and the level of organization, training, and support required for participants to succeed and flourish in their mission. It is grounded in the best practices of pastoral care taught in seminaries and theological schools throughout the country, some simple but profound understandings of modern clinical psychology, the healing wisdom and compassionate care of others that is the central teaching of all the world's great religions, and the more sophisticated lay pastoral care programs that are the hallmarks of lay ministries in several Christian denominations, notably the thorough and highly successful Stephen Ministry widely employed in many Christian faith communities. Not only do these programs provide a highly competent service to their congregants, they also offer a uniquely enriching spiritual experience for their lay pastoral care volunteers, an experience heightened by the depth and thoroughness of the programs.

Lay ministry encompasses two categories of programs. The first includes any program that provides support to congregants without any expectation of repeated contact with a particular needy person. Providing rides for seniors or meals for convalescing members, helping new members acclimate to the church community, or leading support groups would all fall into this category of activities. The second category encompasses just one activity—provision of pastoral care by one church member to another for as long as circumstances require. We will use the term "pastoral care providers" (PCPs) for parishioners who volunteer for this second category of lay ministry. (Congregations have used a variety of titles for these caregivers, such as chaplains, pastoral care associates, or simply lay ministers; this last title is probably least useful, since it doesn't distinguish the special calling and role of these church volunteers.) Any lay ministry program can prove critically important to the life of a church, but providing compassionate and effective pastoral care requires a greater commitment on the part of the volunteer—in time, ongoing training, and supervision. Although we will touch upon programs in the first category, this book focuses on the creation, organization, and maintenance of a church's lay pastoral care program.

This book is organized beginning with an overview—the who, what, where, when, why, and how—of pastoral care (chapter 1). Next, the focus turns to the criteria for and the process of selecting members for the care team (chapter 2). There follows a discussion of two of the three core competencies of lay pastoral care: active listening and awareness of the presence of the sacred (chapter 3). Chapter 4 is devoted to a review of the various strategies in applying the third core competency: assessment. Chapter 5 takes up the organization and management of the pastoral care ministry, including communications and record keeping, and chapter 6 describes approaches to the training and supervision of team members. Finally, the prompting circumstance of many pastoral care encounters—crisis—is explored in chapter 7. The book's appendices contain working documents for implementing a lay ministry program, and there is a comprehensive list of resources for care providers and their supervisors.

A lay pastoral care ministry is different from all other church programs in its foundation in spiritually centered caregiving. It is my hope that with the support and guidance of this volume, ministers and congregants in many congregations will be better equipped to make a thoughtful and productive commitment to expanding their pastoral care services to all of their members.

Note: In keeping with the growing custom of using gender neutral pronouns in printed works when reference is being made to both males or females, I have chosen to use the feminine pronoun throughout this book.

Chapter 1—The Basics

For many years I held a view of humanity that divided people into two categories: those who took care of others and those who did not, the latter being the more aggressive (and always male) movers and shakers who got things done and advanced the world from their leadership positions in all areas of life. I remember first having such thoughts as a boy growing up in Tucson, Arizona. When my best friend, John, and I got together to play, he'd ask, "Do you want to play war?" I'd typically say, "Sure, I'll be the medic," and he'd invariably come back with "I'll be the priest," which, even as an eight-year-old, I thought was a little strange. But what felt really good and made us buddies was that we chose to be this noncombatant team in our war game, ministering to the wounded and dying. Father John got the ones I couldn't fix. Playing war was one of the things you did as a boy back in those days, and I always felt a little out of it being the soldier without a gun until I found a soul mate in John. Then a new house went up near us and brought Ricky into our lives. Ricky was our age but a fighter, both in life and in play. John and I were kind of excited to have a combatant in our game of war, since Ricky could supply a body for us to work on. Meanwhile, my worldview was solidifying; there were basically the tough, fighting people and the wimpier, take-care-of-others sorts, to which group I felt at the time unfortunately drawn. And this is pretty much how I saw the world as I grew up.

As I matured and became more comfortable with the gray areas of life, I began to see considerable crossover between my two groups. But I don't think I completely gave up on my "two types of people" theory until a fellow member of Alcoholics Anonymous (AA) named Leroy changed my thinking. I was still pretty green behind the AA ears, probably a year or so into sobriety, and attended a meeting every day, several of them also attended by Leroy. One of those meetings was known for brawls that regularly broke out in the parking lot and that almost always involved Leroy somewhere near the center. Even if I had been a fighter I would have stayed clear of this man. Leroy was about four inches taller than I and at least a hundred pounds heavier. Regardless of the weather, he wore a sleeveless denim jacket with BORN TO DIE emblazoned across his oxlike back. As far as I could tell, every inch of exposed skin was covered with body art, much of it the sort one acquires in penal institutions. One day I attended a new meeting for me, a huge gathering at noon on a Saturday with hundreds of people in attendance—young, old, babies in arms, dogs, and every conceivable demographic slice of humanity. There were AA and Al-Anon meetings being held simultaneously, and there was a large room given over to day care. I had my ten-year-old daughter with me, so we checked out the day care. There in the middle of the room was Leroy, his enormous body enveloping the two kiddie chairs that were keeping his fanny off the floor, surrounded by dozens of running, screaming kids. With two kids on one knee and three or four others quiet at his feet, he was reading *Clifford the Big Red Dog*—a sight just made to cause a paradigm shift in a beholder. That was the day the world's fighters and wimps became one for me. We are all potential ministers to one another. In fact, I now believe that the drive to be caring is a part of everyone. Its realization in some of us can be inhibited— by neglect, by embracing hurtful values, by existential depression or despair, by drugs and alcohol—but it is there, waiting to be released.

Although I only infrequently ran into Leroy at meetings over the next few years, he was always very friendly to me. I learned from mutual friends that in his biker world Leroy less and less frequently played the role that his appearance signaled, mean and aggressive. Although advancing age and the absence of drugs and alcohol in his life had considerably diminished his lust for head bashing, he was still not someone to cross. But at AA meetings, Leroy was a teddy bear. Apparently, though we all have caregiving in our chemistry, many of us need a setting where it is safe to let that aspect out. Leroy found that space in the halls of twelve-step recovery. Others may find it in their church. Indeed, I do not believe there is a more important reason for the existence of a faith community than to be such a sanctuary in which we can open our hearts to the suffering of others.

How (Where, When, and Why) It Works

This book is about one such opportunity to express in simple but often profound ways our compassionate concern for others. The opportunity is afforded by an active lay ministry program within our church community. As lay ministers we are called to serve our fellow congregants when their lives are overtaken by serious illness, loss, or other painful or threatening circumstances. Not only can it be transformative for individual congregants, such a ministry is fundamental to the integrity and purpose of any community of faith. Here the roots of personal and communal spiritual growth are held and nurtured in the rich soil of service to one another. With the well-being of our congregation in hand, we are ready to bring our message of free religion and our values of interdependence, justice, equality, and inclusion into the broader community. Before we can be prophets in the world, we must learn and practice a thoroughgoing ministry to one another. Not until we are lovingly taking care of all the members of our own church community should we be trooping our banners into the wider world. How we take care of our own will be as powerful a model of faith in action as any social justice programs we can devise.

There are always worthy projects for a church's lay ministry; indeed, there will be at least as many as there are congregants experiencing a need for help. Thus, a lay minister might run an errand or take care of some other task for someone who is temporarily overwhelmed, as with preparation for a daughter's wedding or a loved one's memorial. The need might be for a day of child care while a congregant undergoes a minor surgical procedure. It might mean providing a ride to Sunday services for a church member in a nursing home, or an invitation to Thanksgiving dinner for an elderly congregant with no family nearby. If lay ministers take the time to really engage other members of the congregation, especially those who for some reason might be particularly vulnerable or fragile, they will find opportunities to serve. Engaging others, asking after their health and well-being, looking for hints of needs not being met, such should be standard operating procedure for lay ministers, especially since so many people find it difficult if not impossible to reach out for help without prompting from another. The call to service as a lay minister is a commitment to the intention that no congregant's pastoral needs will ever go unnoticed.

Within a church's lay ministry there is a special, core activity—a ministry with a unique calling in a community of faith. This is the ministry of lay pastoral care provider (PCP). PCPs interact one-on-one with congregants, often over an extended period of time. The commitment of time, self-growth, training, and supervision required of PCPs is different from other volunteer activities in a faith community. While the commitment is substantial, the rewards, both to the church community and to the pastoral care provider, are incalculable.

Before we look at the components of a lay pastoral care program, I want to speak briefly about lay pastoral care in more general terms. To do so I'll steal from a formula used in college journalism classes: In organizing any important story for publication, students must understand the WHO, WHAT, WHERE, WHEN, HOW, and WHY of their subject. For our purposes, we will start with the WHAT.

WHAT is lay pastoral care? As outlined above, pastoral care involves working closely with an individual, family, or special group in the church community to support them in securing their well-being and meet their spiritual needs. For instance, it might mean helping someone coming out of the hospital to identify and secure the resources to get the ongoing social, vocational, or other services needed. It may mean partnering with someone starting the frightening journey to recovery from addiction, a partnership that in itself can be healing. A PCP might become a regular visitor and special friend to a shut-in congregant, providing a caring and compassionate lifeline to the outside world, paying attention to the congregant's health and spirits, perhaps sometimes acting as a go-between with health care providers or distant family members. Pastoral care might mean supporting a mother of young children as she moves through a prolonged and difficult divorce, being a sounding board for ideas, an ear for venting, and a shoulder to cry on. It may mean any of these opportunities and many more, where hope arrives in the selfless, caring presence of another, one who accepts the troubled parishioner in her wholeness just as she is. Lay pastoral care providers represent a tacit understanding that ordained ministers have no corner on the capacity or wherewithal to be of spiritual and emotional comfort to others. More of the WHAT will become evident as we talk about the HOW and WHY.

WHO does lay ministry? As we will see later, there are certain characteristics of personality, character, commitment, and reliability that a person should possess to be considered for this special role. Because of its sensitive nature, this role is usually filled through a careful screening and selection process. Experience shows, however, that many in a faith community possess a combination of attributes that would recommend them for service as pastoral care providers. It can be very useful in the formation of a PCP program to solicit the participation of one or more congregants who have training in health services, such as counselors, social workers, and clinical psychologists. With their expertise and experience they can play an important role in the organization, training, and supervision of the pastoral care providers.

Because the services of pastoral care providers can take many forms, those interested in serving their fellow congregants in this role should seek to identify their gifts —the special ways they may be equipped to contribute to the lay pastoral care program. Some people may prefer to work behind the scenes in support of other PCPs. In one church in New York, Sheila, one of the most active, dedicated, and appreciated lay ministers, keeps the pastoral care visit records in good up-to-date order; she also serves as a librarian for the PCPs' collection of printed and video resources. Sheila has found that keeping the pastoral care resource library up to date on information about local health care providers, health-related meetings and events in the community, twelve-step meetings, and so forth requires a commitment of time and attention. In the relatively small church where she is a member, her enthusiasm and expertise are indispensable to the functioning of the lay pastoral care program (and indeed to the church's entire lay ministry program in all its activities). She has also become a visible representative of the church in the community as she gathers the resources that support her church's lay pastoral care initiatives. Indeed, several new members of her church were introduced to it through dealings with Sheila, who, picking up on their interest in liberal religion, invited them to come to Sunday worship. When

Sheila first was asked about lay pastoral care, she dismissed it out of hand. Why? She was too shy, she felt, to work with congregants one on one. But she found her niche. As Sheila's story suggests, there are many ways to serve in a pastoral care program. Invariably, one of the most exciting aspects of the organization of such a program is just this process of discovery, encouraging and supporting members in looking deep within themselves for their special gifts.

WHEN and WHERE do lay pastoral care ministers provide their services? It is tempting to reply, wherever and whenever there is a congregant in need of support and attention. And for the most part this is the case. Most commonly, though, pastoral care encounters will transpire at church, in the congregant's home, or in a health care facility such as a nursing home, hospital, or hospice. Quite often, a PCP will be approached on Sunday morning at coffee hour, and if such is the case, the PCP will seek out a quiet place at church or agree to meet later. It is also sometimes necessary to coordinate pastoral calls with a congregant's family member or caregiver or to take into consideration the visiting hours of a health care facility. When and how pastoral care providers engage with congregants should be important focuses in the organization of a church's lay pastoral care program. However initial contact is made, thereafter the pastoral care provider can set the rules about when she will be available to be contacted and how that contact should be made (for instance, whether she wants to be contacted on a personal phone or prefers communication to go through a central church contact). As a pastoral care relationship develops, the dynamics will change, and the question of how, where, and under what circumstances a PCP makes herself available to a congregant can be revisited and fine-tuned.

HOW is a lay pastoral care ministry carried out? It may take many forms. Ultimately, how it's done is however it needs to be done, given the scope and resources of a particular church. That's why it's so important to muster a variety of folks to do this work. The activities may differ, but most often, whatever the effort, at its heart is a very simple gesture—making oneself available to another who is suffering and sharing the load through compassionate, nonjudgmental presence. PCPs bring no agenda of their own other than to be of help. They do not try to fix a difficult personal problem or proffer advice. Do you know the criteria for the giving of advice to be successful? The person you want to give advice to must

1. need advice
2. know she needs advice
3. want advice
4. want advice from you
5. want advice from you at that moment

The likelihood that all five of these criteria will be met in any given situation is precariously close to zero. Suffering people often just want us to care enough to be there. In their distress they aren't looking to an MD or a marriage counselor or a CPA. They are not looking for advice, a cure, textbook wisdom, or other authoritative pronouncements. The yearning in their heart is for a compassionate companion whose presence they can count on no matter how difficult things get, another human being like themselves whose presence—even in silence, perhaps just holding their hand, perhaps singing a song or making soup—makes this commitment: "I will be with you. You will not be alone." Simple presence is the great gift we have to offer as pastoral care providers. It is a gift that can and has changed people's lives.

WHY a pastoral care ministry? Among all the other ways in which lay pastoral care enriches the personal and community experience of church life, it has a very practical reason for existence. Even in a small church, it is impossible for the church pastor to minister at every moment to everyone with a need. Every church requires a pastoral care program to supplement the care provided by the professional staff. There will be people who do not think their problem is serious enough to bring to the minister or who won't be comfortable speaking to the minister about a particular problem, but they might be comfortable bringing that problem to a lay care provider. There will be people in need whom the pastor will be unaware of and who are in danger of being invisible. But the additional eyes and ears of the lay care providers tremendously reduce this possibility. In the church where I first trained as a lay care provider, there were roughly 380 members and one minister, and the PCPs served the congregation with considerable distinction. When the minister took a yearlong sabbatical, no part-time minister for pastoral care was hired. The lay PCPs had the trust and respect of the congregation and filled in without a hitch (they *did* have an on-call minister available to them for advice and referral if needed, but as I remember such a call was never made). Simply put, PCPs extend the reach of the ordained ministry in the church, ensuring that no member in need is left unattended.

In addition, we are called by our principles and by the traditions of our liberal religious movement to a lay ministry of pastoral care. To act upon our belief in the worth and dignity of every human being does not require a search in some far-off third world country for people who are hurt, sick, or in some other way needing our services. Such folks sit next to us every Sunday in our pews. Often their pain is concealed, but it is there, uncommunicated. There will be congregants—friends— who are experiencing job loss, divorce or other relational upheaval, substance abuse, the death or slow decline of a loved one. We may never learn about these troubling circumstances until we prepare ourselves as a church to discover and respond to each such person. And we will need multiple response systems, since no parish minister can handle all the pain and suffering in her congregation, especially among those who suffer protracted or chronic health challenges that require ongoing, long-term attention. Our church can be a place of sanctuary and hope for all our fellow members as we ourselves develop our capacity to serve one another through an active lay pastoral care program. The promise we make in embracing such a program is as meaningful a commitment as a human being can make: We accept responsibility for the well-being of every person in our church. No one who seeks it will go without our compassionate concern and support. If we truly believe in the worth and dignity of every person, we are obliged to consider the needs, the very local needs, of our fellow congregants.

Finally, there is one more WHY. Life offers us no greater gift than the opportunity to care for another. I had a psychotherapy professor who used to say that we do not become adults until we take responsibility for the well-being of another. The ministry of lay pastoral care is a path to an ever-deepening personal spiritual growth, growth that is just an illusion without a cultivation of the habit of reaching out to others.

Chapter 2—Selecting Members of the Pastoral Care Team

One of the goals of any lay ministry program is to model the sort of concern and support for our fellow human beings that all of us can practice in our daily encounters with one another. There is no one in the congregation who can't deepen the quality of her relationships with others through a conscious effort to be more caring and other-focused. Indeed, there is undoubtedly some formal lay ministry role for many members of a congregation, and in any one of these roles there would be opportunity for personal growth. But among all the volunteer opportunities in a faith community, including lay ministry, the role of lay pastoral care provider is unique in the combination of character and commitment that a person must bring to the work. It is a spiritual calling that entails significant responsibilities, responsibilities to one's care receivers, minister, congregation, and personal well-being. There will always be people in the congregation who are equipped to function as PCPs but who can't make the time commitment or whose work as caregivers outside the church community will prompt them to seek other ways to contribute to the church. In creating a pastoral care program, it is also important that the cadre of PCPs represent as much as possible the diversity of the congregation. In the interests of reflecting this diversity, some qualified church members will choose to wait for the normal turnover in lay ministry participation to provide openings for them on the pastoral care team. Meanwhile, the selection of the members of the church's lay pastoral care team should be undertaken with thoughtfulness and concern for the sensibility and responsibilities borne by the PCP.

Speaking of diversity, it was not unusual twenty-five years ago for a response to a call for lay pastoral providers to attract a number of women and only the occasional man. It is tempting to attribute this imbalance to an assumption about those days that women were still seen as the nurturers with an innate call to caregiving, while men were required to develop a degree of callousness toward others' feelings (and their own) in order to be successful breadwinners. But men did come forward, and the numbers seemed to increase slowly over the years. The earliest male volunteers were invariably older men who were finding a need in retirement to create meaning in their lives, a goal that they discovered couldn't be realized through endless rounds of golf and hands of canasta. In ministering to fellow congregants they began to experience the meaningfulness of acts of compassionate care. Increasingly, younger men are being attracted to the work of pastoral care, but they are typically still outnumbered by women. This situation is unfortunate not only because men are missing out on the opportunity to experience the spiritual growth and personal satisfaction afforded by this volunteer activity, but also because there will always be parishioners (both male and female) who would prefer male care providers, as well as care recipients for whom a male caregiver could be most effective, e.g., fatherless male youth and young adults. Meanwhile, it can be an effective strategy to have the minister seek out male congregants with the requisite character and interests and personally invite them to join the pastoral care team. It is worth making a special effort to achieve gender balance on the pastoral care team: Male care providers who exhibit such qualities as compassion, emotional vulnerability, and gentleness can be powerful models to other male congregants in overcoming stereotypes of masculinity. Similar barriers may keep men from other church activities, such as involvement in the religious education program. As male participation in such programs grows, more men will be freed from the constraints that have kept them from yielding to their hearts' urging to reach out empathically to others.

How many PCPs should a church have? There is no perfect formula for finding this number, although experience suggests that a team of four to six people in a small-to-medium-size church and up to eight in a large church is a workable number. Another rule of thumb is to grow the lay ministry until there is one PCP for every fifty church members. However, to reiterate, whatever the number of participants, the team should include representation of the church's largest demographic constituencies, beginning with gender, age, and race. This is certainly doable in a PCP team as small as four members. It is also important to emphasize that even with a small group of PCPs, any one care provider may go for a considerable period of time without being directly contacted for help by a congregant. The existence of a lay pastoral care ministry, however, bears a significance for a congregation that far outweighs the number of contacts made by the pastoral care team. That a congregation chooses to establish and support such a ministry program in itself will bring comfort to many. The community that raises a team of lay pastoral care providers makes a profound religious commitment to the well-being of all its members, and that commitment itself will become foundational in the faith community's understanding of its mission and goals. Meanwhile, the church pastor will usually be able to identify congregants with special needs that will keep the PCPs actively engaged in their calling.

Typically, the parish minister will select the pastoral care team based on her knowledge of the personalities and characters of church members.

Personality Qualities of the PCP

When we started our lay ministry program at my church in 1985, one of the four folks who was chosen by our minister to be trained was an older woman I'll call Anna. Anna was a Russian Jew who had lost close family members in the Holocaust. She was a pretty tough, no-nonsense lady with a huge heart that she seemed to try to hide with her gruff exterior. Although we had an ongoing program of training to help us grow as lay ministers, Anna never changed in the slightest way her procedure with people who asked for help. If you weren't well, or were lonely or troubled, whatever it was, Anna would come to your house, start a pot of chicken soup, look for an afghan to put on your lap, and then announce she was going to putter. "Now you just rest there and eat that good soup. I'll just putter around the house." No matter what the problem was, that was Anna's ministerial response. When we tried to expand her helping repertoire, she would dismiss us with a wave of the hand, an "Ach!," and a scowl. A fact that wasn't lost on the rest of us was that Anna quickly became the go-to lay minister. And for very good reason. She provided in spades the most fundamental gift of lay ministry, presence—compassionate, nonjudgmental presence. It didn't matter who the person or what the problem was, her presence said, "No matter what, I'm going to be here with you. You're not going to be alone." Our presence is the Bayer aspirin of ministering to others —it takes care of so many of the emotional and spiritual aches and pains that can beset one's life. If we are not alone we can have hope, hope that things will change, hope that things will get better.

Have you ever noticed that there are certain people in your congregation whose personality and demeanor make you feel comfortable and listened-to when you're in their presence? If pressed to describe their effect on us, we might characterize their presence as ministerial or pastoral. And we might have sensed that presence even before we interacted with them, before they demonstrated the skills of an effective care provider. Are there certain aspects of character or personality traits that tend to give us the security to be vulnerable and at the same time hopeful for gentle, nonjudgmental support and guidance? The following list of traits is not meant to be exhaustive or rigidly adhered to in judging a person's suitability for lay pastoral ministry. However, it is representative of the attributes that seem to draw us to certain others in a time of need.

1. **Emotionally stable.** Good psychological health would seem to be an obvious qualification for working closely with congregants who are suffering, but it is important to make this point explicitly for this reason: The role of pastoral care provider often attracts some of the most psychologically needy members of a congregation. For such congregants, despite their best intentions, providing pastoral care will always be more about them than the care recipient. Their ability to remain calm and focused, not to mention maintaining strong personal boundaries, will always be threatened by their own emotional fragility. Ironically, if such members were able to acknowledge their own needs, they themselves could very well be good prospects to receive pastoral care. Typically, no psychological screening test is necessary to identify these folks. Their actions and comportment within the congregation will have signaled their neediness. Very occasionally, however, the personal problems of such congregants may only emerge as they undertake a pastoral care role. It is therefore necessary for the parish minister and the lay PCPs to be vigilant for evidence of such problematic behavior and to intervene with compassion to end a congregant's participation on the pastoral care team if that behavior emerges. Such an intervention may provide an opportunity for the minister, through supportive counseling, to motivate a needy church member to seek appropriate professional care.

2. **Empathic.** Perhaps the single most important quality that a PCP will bring to the caregiving role is empathy—the readiness to walk in another's shoes.

We can feel sorry for people, pity them, be sympathetic to their plight, all the while maintaining our distance. But the empathic person hears the singular, simple, and often silent cry of the heart: "Please come to me; please be with me; please walk with me." The empathic person understands that congregants in crisis hope for her attention and presence. Their need is for the PCP to leave the comfort of her world to join them where they are and then walk with them through their time of trial. This joining is unlikely to require significant physical presence in the life of another. More often, it will be a journey of the mind and spirit, a joining in which the goal is insignificant compared to the promise of companionship on the way. Such a journey may be, at various times, heartbreaking, joyous, perplexing, mindless, mindful—all the emotions and experiences of a full life. Such a journey requires PCPs to be both courageous and vulnerable as they walk the walk of partnership and loving-kindness. Saying yes to this invitation to come into another's life is the essential act of a pastoral care provider; being capable of such partnering is the irreducible minimum requirement for becoming a PCP.

3. **A good listener.** If the primary personal quality of the PCP is the ability to be present to another in times of difficulty, the primary activity in such circumstances is the deceptively simple act of listening. But the listening that is healing for a troubled person is very different from the sort of listening most of us do most of the time. Typically we listen to another with half an ear: Our mind wanders to our own preoccupations or,

after hearing a bit of what another is telling us, we mentally disengage in order to begin formulating our response. As a result, we rarely hear all that a person is telling us, and the speaker rarely feels heard. Good listening skills, summed up in the expression "active listening," require our full attention. Remember, the empathic journey requires us to leave our world, including our self-centered thoughts, and move into the other's world. So our listening becomes what it rarely is without practice and intention: other centered. Active listening goes hand in hand with empathic presence, and people who tend to be attentive listeners, able to put aside their own agenda to be in the moment and focused on the needs of another, possess one of the most critical qualities for being an effective PCP.

4. **Nonjudgmental.** I was once a chaplain to a hospice patient dying of pancreatitis and end-stage liver disease, the consequences of a life of alcoholic drinking. Our hospice team was supplementing the care the patient was receiving in a nursing home, and I arrived at his room one day to find him sitting in his wheelchair, hunched over with pain. When I asked the supervising nurse about getting the patient medicine for his pain, I was told, "He is an alcoholic; the medicine will just feed his habit. Besides, it probably won't do any good, since he's built up so much tolerance." Through the intervention of our hospice medical director, the patient soon was made comfortable, and the next day our hospice pain specialist did an in-service training for the nursing home staff. But I'm not sure that even this very

thorough training session changed that particular nurse's mind. She had made a judgment about her patient and his lifestyle. As far as she was concerned, he was responsible for the situation he now found himself in—a street person dying in a nursing home from self-abuse. She had more worthy patients to attend to. Such prejudice has no place in ministry. Our calling is to meet people in crisis where they are and then try to imagine how they are feeling. From that empathetic viewpoint we can best discover what they need to find well-being. In this effort, it is not useful to hold up any aspect of their life as a moral lesson. Our faith calls us to a belief in the worth and dignity of every human being, not just likable human beings, or human beings who live their lives the way we suppose they should. A nonjudgmental approach to our caregiving responsibilities can be challenging, especially given the many prejudices that are culturally ingrained in us. But lay ministry gives us the opportunity to suspend these prejudices by seeing the world through another's eyes and brain and heart. Indeed, in this way we may feel most poignantly the prejudices that torment others (and recognize prejudice in ourselves). In our search for candidates to become PCPs, we should be alert to folks who are not quick to judgment but instead tend to allow other people to be who they are, coming to them with no distracting preconceptions about the relative value of their lives or what they may need from us.

5. **Humble.** Humility is often misunderstood in our competitive and acquisitive society. Some people equate humility with weakness and timidity, servility,

even humiliation. But the concept of humility has ancient origins and in its long history has often been understood as a virtue—one that embodies gentleness, modesty, patience, and an acceptance of ourselves just as we are, with all our strengths and failings. It is the preeminent fact of our humanity that each of us is both saint and sinner. And the humble are comfortable at the balance point in this contradiction. By accepting ourselves in both our strengths and weaknesses, we are more likely to tolerate the same muddled package in others.

There are several practical implications that derive from our understanding of our own weaknesses and strengths. If we understand the circumstances in which we can't be helpful to another—whether due to the lack of specialized knowledge, experience, or personal vulnerabilities—we can be prepared to refer a congregant to someone who can help. Indeed, this may be the very reason we have been sought out: We are seen as a trusted ally in the search for appropriate help. (Such situations emphasize the importance for the pastoral care provider of an ongoing effort at familiarization with community care providers and other resources for our congregants.) On the other side of the humility equation, PCPs must understand their strengths. They must also understand that strength brings power and authority. Whenever someone seeks help from another, the power balance tips toward the care provider: When that authority is ceded to us, we must hold it with great care. Our pastoral duty calls us to share our strength, empowering our care recipients to regain a sense of hope and control in their lives. People arrive at hopelessness through helplessness, and it is in finding the strength to act effectively on their own behalf — to understand where and how they can again bring direction to their life — that healing and growth take place. But the authority in a caregiving relationship can be abused, wittingly or unwittingly keeping one's care recipient in thrall to feed one's ego. The PCP must be vigilant, therefore, in regularly taking the measure of the power dynamics in every caring relationship.

6. **Available.** On the one hand, being available means making oneself accessible to one's care recipients when they are in need of support. However, being available does not mean being on call twenty-four hours a day, seven days a week. It means collaborating on a schedule of availability that meets the needs of one's care recipients while respecting one's other responsibilities. It means being faithful to this schedule once it is established. But availability also implies a more subtle readiness to open one's heart to another. It is this opening that leads to empathy and the possibility of a deep understanding of the hurt or confusion another is feeling. In each pastoral encounter, our availability asserts our desire and readiness to walk another's path with her. If we find ourselves distracted and struggling to engage with the other when we are meeting, we are not making ourselves available.

7. **Dependable.** As anybody who has spent any time in a faith community or other volunteer organization appreciates, volunteerism is a double-edged sword.

The ability to come forth and share their resources—experience, time, skills—with those in need is a precious gift enthusiastically offered by many volunteers. But some people's hearts are so big that they just can't seem to say no. The venerable 80-20 rule certainly is at work in our churches: 80 percent of the work gets done by 20 percent of the people, and usually the same people over and over again, year in and year out, until they burn out and go underground for a few years. Despite their best intentions, it is simply impossible for these folks to do justice to all the obligations that they take on. And we must acknowledge that there is a small number of folks who for whatever reason cannot be counted on to do what they say they will do. Not surprisingly, congregants in either of these two categories are not good prospects for the PCP team. (It is not uncommon for a person in the first category to give up other obligations in order to concentrate on pastoral care, and their ministries can be successful, although they may find it difficult to resist backsliding, especially after they feel they have "figured out" the role of PCP; such folks may be helped by their peers in supervision to respect their commitments as pastoral care providers.) Dependability in members of the pastoral care team extends to their responsibilities to their fellow PCPs. Regular participation in supervisory sessions is an obligation that each PCP should honor.

8. **Circumspect.** Try though they might, many people just find it impossible to keep a secret: "I'd never tell a soul... I do share everything with my spouse, but she isn't even a member of the church. Other than her..."

Some people are such established cogs in the rumor mill that expectations either on our part or theirs that they will be able to hold a confidence are downright foolish. Given their positive qualities, there can be other jobs for such folks in lay ministry, but not as PCPs. Indeed, a breach of confidentiality on the part of just one PCP can threaten the congregation's feeling of safety dealing with any of the PCPs. Though no human being can be expected always and forever to be respectful of every confidence shared with her, it is certainly possible to exclude some folks in the PCP selection process who have given us little confidence in this regard. Even after thoughtful selections of PCP candidates are made within this context, confidentiality should be a topic often revisited in both ongoing training and supervision.

9. **Presentable.** One would think that being presentable would not need mentioning, but unfortunately, in today's "dress-down" society, understanding the effect on others of the way we dress and groom ourselves seems to be too frequently absent. A pastoral care encounter is a serious event, and one's respect for that fact is at least in part reflected in how one physically presents oneself. This may be especially significant in caring for seniors who were raised in an era when how one presented oneself demonstrated one's respect for the meaning of an occasion and the sensibilities of the others involved. This is certainly not a call for formal attire in making pastoral calls, but it is a reminder that our thoughtfulness is at least in part reflected in how we prepare ourselves for a visit. Lay ministers are not professional care

providers, but the training and supervision that informs their work should not be sabotaged by a less than respectful physical appearance.

10. **Committed to the pastoral care program.** Becoming a PCP requires a substantial commitment of time—with one's care receivers, one's peers, and in the solitary work of reflection and preparation for the various aspects of this work. Some folks' professional lives are simply too strenuous and time-consuming, or too unpredictable, to allow them to make the commitments required of the PCP. Over time, PCPs should expect to grow—in effectiveness as well as personal spiritual well-being—as they gain experience in the role. They should therefore be expected to make a commitment of several years to their ministry. Thus, if someone knows she will be moving from the community in the near future, she should be discouraged from pursuing a place on the pastoral care team. Similarly, people who take regular vacations (here in the Northeast we have a sizable flock of "snowbirds" who decamp for southern climes to escape New England winters) often find it more difficult to be faithful to their commitments as PCPs. Sometimes, in larger churches with sizable pastoral care programs, a PCP can team with a fellow care provider to share a commitment to a care receiver, and such partnerships occasionally work. But missing peer supervision and regular interactions with the congregation can diminish one's ability to stay current with the church's pastoral care needs and interrupt the continuity of one's growth as a lay minister.

11. **Committed to self-care and maintaining strong personal boundaries.** We have all known caregivers who will drop everything to respond to a person in need. Such selflessness is often admirable, but it can be a serious drawback if carried to extremes, i.e., if it is allowed to erode the interpersonal boundaries that help a person maintain her own emotional and spiritual health as distinct from that of the care receiver. The rate of burnout is high in the caregiving professions, and it seems that all too often caregivers either don't recognize or ignore the signs of overinvolvement with their care recipients. Effective PCPs will be able to say no to a call for help if they are feeling exhausted, overwhelmed, or overcommitted. In order to be responsible in such circumstances, PCPs should be prepared to make a referral to another caregiver. But their first duty is to see to their own well-being. Cultivating strong interpersonal boundaries, insisting on time for rest and recreation in one's daily schedule, and maintaining a personal spiritual practice are among the activities that can ensure well-being and the vigor necessary to be an effective pastoral care provider. Candidates for PCP should embrace such elements of self-care, respecting the wisdom that sometimes saying no is the best medicine for all concerned.

Respecting the integrity of our own personal boundaries implicitly carries the obligation to recognize and honor the personal boundaries of those who come to us for care in times of trauma or stress. Our care recipients may be susceptible to a dependence on our attention that can undermine their self-efficacy—their sense of control over their own life. Thus, trying to fix their problems can contribute to the vulnerability of their sense of self brought about by their suffering, while supporting them in finding their own solutions to their problems can strengthen the healthy boundaries that preserve their individuality.

12. **Active in life of church; familiar with liberal religious theologies, history, and polity.** PCPs should be church members with at least a two-year history of engagement in the life of the church, including committee work, volunteering in youth or adult religious education programs, etc. They should have knowledge of the important events in their church community's history as well as an understanding of liberal religious and its history, theologies, and congregational polity. Knowledge in all these areas can be honed in ongoing PCP training sessions, but a basic familiarity with the history of the liberal religious movement should be an entry-level requirement for participation in the church's lay pastoral care program.

13. **Familiar with church's "code of conduct" rules.** Most churches have in place a code of conduct for ministerial and non-ministerial staff and volunteers. Such a document will have been approved and adopted by the church's governing board. All PCPs should be familiar with the details of this or other similar document and hold themselves accountable to its rules and recommendations.

As mentioned earlier, the church pastor will usually be the person most familiar with individual congregants' character and personality traits. She will therefore be equipped to make the most informed selections for the pastoral care team. The above outline of desirable personal qualities and commitments can support the selection process. Publishing such a list within the congregation may help everyone understand the high standards and expectations that will characterize the pastoral care team's ministry and provide aspirants to the pastoral care role with a yardstick for self-assessment.

Once chosen, the new pastoral care team will require training in the core competencies of lay pastoral care. In the next two chapters we will look closely at these essential skills.

Chapter 3—Core Competencies: Active Listening and Awareness of the Presence of the Sacred

While working with people in distress or crisis may require a variety of responses from the PCP, there are three essential skills that will be called upon in every caring encounter. Obtaining these skills can be seen as the minimum requirement to ensuring that a care encounter will be supportive and healing. These—the three As of pastoral care—are: active listening, awareness of the sacred, and assessment. Ongoing training will give PCPs many tools that will prove useful in various circumstances, but acquiring the three As should precede a PCP's first pastoral encounter. Thereafter, they should be continuously revisited and one's grasp of them reassessed, both in personal reflection and in supervision with one's peers. The essentials of these skills are not complicated, but they may feel unnatural—while we may understand the value they would bring to our day-to-day lives and to our ministries, they are not typically practiced in our routine interpersonal relationships. These skills will not only form the foundational praxis of our pastoral ministries; we may find that they are transformative in the quality of our daily interactions with others as well.

When a PCP is first contacted by a congregant, the congregant is informed that the fact of the congregant's reaching out to the lay care provider will be shared with the parish minister. Beyond that, whatever is said between them will be held in confidence. If the PCP judges that the congregant's concern may require discussion with the minister or with the other PCPs in supervision, the congregant should be informed that there are two exceptions to the rule of confidentiality. First, the PCP will disclose information for which she feels the advice of the minister or her fellow PCPs is critical—with the minister the congregant's name will be shared; with the PCP's supervisory group, the congregant may choose to have her name and any identifying details omitted. Second, the PCP must communicate with the minister or appropriate professional if the congregant implies that she plans to hurt herself or another or reports knowing of someone who has been hurt or who plans to hurt another. If the congregant cannot agree with these possible exceptions to the confidentiality of the interaction with a PCP, then the PCP can provided assistance to the congregant in seeking professional advice and support. When the rules of confidentiality have been understood and accepted, the PCP can begin work with the care receiver.

If, as is often the case, initial contact is made at Sunday morning coffee hour or another church function, the PCP should suggest finding a private location where the congregant can speak openly without worrying about being overheard. If such a location is unavailable at the time, the PCP can suggest a meeting elsewhere, a home visit, or a telephone conversation. Whatever the congregant's choice, the lack of privacy at coffee hour always makes such a venue inappropriate for a pastoral care visit.

Active Listening

Not arbitrarily, we begin with the art of listening. There are no scientific studies on the relative importance of the various skills that are employed in providing pastoral care. But experience affirms that listening, just listening to another, is by far the most important activity of the pastoral care provider. Indeed, it is probably safe to say that all other components of pastoral care combined will take up no more than 10 percent of the caregiver's time. But the listening we refer to here is of a different quality from what most of us routinely practice. *Active listening*, the term most often used to refer to it, is indeed an art, one that we can learn, practice, and get better at to the benefit of ourselves and those with whom we interact. In contrast to our more typical pattern of passively and usually quite inattentively receiving information from another, active listening requires us to be fully, actively engaged in the listening process—to do listening, if you will, rather than be a listener. The following advice, attributed variously to Dr. Ralph Broughton and to other anonymous sources, eloquently captures the thrust of active listening:

> When I ask you to listen to me and you start giving advice, you have not done what I asked. When I ask you to listen to me and you begin to tell me why I shouldn't feel that way, you are trampling on my feelings. When I ask you to listen to me and you feel you must do something to solve my problems, you have failed me, strange as that may seem.
>
> Listen! All I asked was that you listen. Not talk or do—just hear me. Advice is cheap: ten cents will get you both Dear Abby and Billy Graham in the same

newspaper. And I can do for myself: I'm not helpless, maybe discouraged and faltering, but not helpless. When you do something for me that I can and need to do for myself, you contribute to my fear and weakness.

But when you accept as a simple fact that I do feel what I feel, no matter how irrational, then I quit trying to convince you and can get about the business of understanding what's behind the irrational feeling. And when that's clear, the answers are obvious and I don't need advice.

Irrational feelings make sense when we understand what's behind them.

Perhaps that's why prayer works, sometimes, for some people, because God is mute, and he doesn't give advice or try to fix things. He just listens and lets you work it out for yourself.

So please listen and just hear me, and, if you want to talk, wait a minute for your turn, and I'll listen to you.

The qualities of active listening, several of which are alluded to in this passage, include the following:

1. We are fully focused on the speaker, not ourselves. In a typical conversation, we usually hear only a little of what our partner has to say before we begin tuning out in order to formulate our response. Once we have shifted our attention to our own thoughts we are no longer hearing the other person. In active listening, our primary goal is to really hear all of what the other is telling us. To this end, we actively let go of judgments, conclusions, or devising solutions to a problem being presented to us. Since our goal is only

to understand what the other is saying, any questions we might have will involve seeking clarification for some comment that we don't understand. We can test our understanding by rephrasing what we have just been told and inviting the speaker to correct any misunderstanding on our part.

2. We are not judgmental or critical of what a person has to say, nor do we attempt to solve the problem or issue at hand. Indeed, we are trying, through our attentiveness, to put ourselves in our care receiver's shoes, sharing in both the meaning of what she is saying and the feelings she is expressing.

3. We convey our attentiveness in several ways:

    a. by our posture (relaxed and open—no arms folded across our chest or body turned to one side)
    b. by maintaining eye contact
    c. by our occasional head nods and interjections of "hmm" or "I see"
    d. by our disregard of distractions (we do not answer a call on our cell phone if we have forgotten to turn it off before we began our listening)
    e. by resisting our impulse to finish sentences or interrupt with personal opinions or analysis
    f. by not interrupting our partner with questions that force her into a new line of thought

4. We try not to show signs of upset or irritation.

5. We pay attention to the speaker's body language, which may at times be more indicative of her feelings than her words are: the casting down of the gaze in

sadness or shame, the welling of tears in the eyes, the inability to make or sustain eye contact, the leaning inward toward us or the pulling back. While the meaning of such signs may be clouded, we know that they are inflecting the speaker's words and adding nuance to what we are being told. We wait patiently for the speaker to articulate the message behind these subtle signs.

6. We learn to sit with silences. Interludes of silence are always important to a speaker. They may indicate the speaker's search for the important next thing to say, or consideration of what she has just said; i.e., in the telling of her story she heard something new and important about herself, her problems, or the way she feels, and she needs some moments to make sense of this awareness. Becoming comfortable with silence is very important for the PCP, not only for these reasons but also because it may be the nature of some of our pastoral care encounters that very little is spoken. In such cases, it may simply be the PCP's attentive presence that brings comfort and healing to a care recipient. The silences in our encounters are always meaningful. Unfortunately, in our hurry-up society, we have become uncomfortable with and disrespectful of the nurturing power of silence and are too quickly inclined to rush in with meaningless talk.

7. We observe our own feelings. Being attentive to our care recipient's words does not mean that the import or tenor of her message won't sometimes arouse strong feelings in us. Indeed, some level of feeling is quite typical. We can be focused on the speaker and

still be sensitive to our own feelings, especially negative ones. Indeed, the capacity to monitor the intensity of our internal reactions to what is being said to us is an indispensable component of the art of active listening. Our feelings can run a wide gamut as we began our work as PCPs. Such feelings may be mild—no more than a case of the jitters: "Am I doing this right?" "I hope I'm prepared for what might happen here." But they may also be extreme, the latter thankfully being a rare occurrence. In such cases we notice that we are very upset: Thoughts and feelings are coming up that are overwhelming us. The pastoral encounter is not the context in which to analyze such feelings, and when such feelings arise, the PCP must end the encounter and seek help—from the minister or other supervisor or a more seasoned PCP. We can think of the range of intensity of our feelings as notches on a thermometer, from cool ("I'm noticing some negative feelings, but they are not distracting me"), through warm ("I am beginning to feel a bit uncomfortable with this conversation, but having noted that, I can relax, take a deep breath, and return to listening"), to hot ("I need to stop now"). Monitoring our level of anxiety in pastoral encounters is really not difficult, but it requires intention—a routine, brief checking-in with oneself as a pastoral encounter unfolds.

Movement on the discomfort thermometer from warm to hot is usually gradual, and therefore it is possible to be prepared to end the meeting. Sometimes, however, our care recipient may say something that immediately causes us to flounder: Beyond this point we know we will not be able to focus on the other. Some such messages can be prepared for. For instance, a PCP may encounter someone who announces that she has been having suicidal thoughts. Knowing that suicidal thinking is one of the concerns that may prompt a congregant to seek out a PCP, we will be prepared with a response and therefore be able to maintain our composure. But when a care recipient touches something deeply disturbing inside us, we must be prepared to say, "I'm sorry, but I need to end our meeting. I don't think I can be helpful to you right now. But I will call you later. If you need to speak with someone immediately, I can refer you to another PCP or to our minister." Any incidents of anxiety should be processed with the minister, in supervision, or both.

Active listening involves all of these qualities, and role-playing these skills is usually a high point of lay pastoral care training sessions (for active-listening role-play, see chapter 6). As with learning any new skill, competence and confidence in active listening will grow over time.

Awareness of the Presence of the Sacred
People who seek out pastoral care providers typically have a sense that their issues have a spiritual component —something to do with their deepest values and beliefs. Thus, the way they understand themselves, others, or life itself in its mysteriousness has been challenged by a personal experience. The result is a sense of spiritual crisis or disorientation. The congregant has lost a loved one, and this loss challenges her sense of the fairness of life, or she has been victimized by societal prejudice,

deeply disturbing her sense of safety and security in the world. These are spiritual experiences. Indeed, most of the issues that people bring to a pastoral care provider can be seen as a threat to one's sense of one's goodness; the goodness, compassion, and caring of others; or the inherent goodness of the world around us.

In seminary, ministerial pastoral-care-providers-in-training are taught to ask these questions: Where is God in our encounter with a troubled person? How is God acting in our relationship with our care recipient? How is the life force active just now in our pastoral encounter? Put another way, God is always the third presence in our one-to-one sessions with another. As humanists, we might see the presence of loving-kindness in our encounters, the force for ever-increasing good in the world as a collaborator in our efforts in caring for a troubled soul. We can ask our care recipients about their spirituality, their faith, the values and beliefs they hold most dearly. Whatever their theology, we should be prepared to help them access the strength that they may derive from their faith—a connection perhaps forgotten or unseeable in the turmoil of their circumstances. We might expect a Christian to ask us to pray with her, but such a request from a humanist should not surprise us. In our distress, it is not uncommon for us to reach back to the faith of our family of origin, the beliefs and rituals that comforted our parents and perhaps ourselves as children. As an example, I once visited a congregant in a nursing home who was convalescing from cancer surgery. She had been an active church member for many years, often participating in church events sponsored by the congregation's humanist group, and in our many interactions I had never seen any evidence that her spirituality was God centered. On this particular day, I came into her room and noticed a framed picture of Jesus on the nightstand next to her bed. After a few minutes of chatting, I asked, tentatively, if she would like me to pray with her, and she said, with great relief in her eyes, "Oh, would you?" She then referred to her Catholic upbringing and with a little self-deprecating humor allowed as how when things get tough, one wants to cover all of one's bets. Given her health problems, she had no need to hide the fact that she found comfort in the spirituality of her youth. And so we prayed, she holding my hand with a strong, sure grasp. In training as a PCP, we are well advised to prepare ourselves to pray with a fellow congregant or her family. There are several resources in the bibliography at the end of this book that can be very useful to the liberally religious care provider needing to respond to a congregant who seeks comfort in a Christian, Jewish, Buddhist, Native American, or other faith tradition.

Pastoral care often brings us up against a theological issue that has proved historically difficult for people in the liberal religious tradition. The question of evil or suffering in the world is one we have managed largely to avoid in our long history. Eighteenth- and nineteenth-century American Unitarianism emphasized the seemingly inexorable evolution of human prosperity and the realization of personal spiritual awakening. In the early twentieth century there was much attention given to the potential for one world religion to bring disparate societies together in a common spiritual bond. At the same time, the rise of secular humanism presaged an age of social and economic progress in which people everywhere would come ever closer to realizing their full human potential. This was the faith that was preached on Sundays from Unitarian pulpits, and the question of evil seemed rarely to arise. (This was also the era in which the number of American Unitarians reached its peak.) But then the horrors of World War II, the Holocaust, and the atom bomb stunned us with the spectacle of human beings' extraordinary capacity for barbarity. For the first time in our history, we Unitarians couldn't avoid trying to make sense of suffering in the world. We were ill-equipped, and to this day, Unitarian Universalist theology struggles mightily with this reality.

As pastoral care providers, we are often beckoned into the lives of people burdened by great suffering, and our capacity to partner with them through their suffering requires that we, individually, come to grips with this hard fact of life. (Again, please refer to the bibliography for resources on this subject.) It can be very helpful and healing to ask our care recipients, in the context of a discussion about their spirituality, how they understand suffering and its meaning to them. In preparation for this discussion, it behooves us to ask the same question of ourselves. We should be prepared to meet this subject head-on in working with our care recipients. As it becomes relevant, this subject can also usefully be the focus of PCP training and discussions in supervisory sessions.

Familiarity with active listening and an awareness of the sacred lay the groundwork for the next step in the pastoral care of troubled parishioners: assessment of their issues and building a plan to address those issues. In the next chapter we will explore this critical pastoral care skill.

Chapter 4—Core Competencies: Assessment

Being able to help a troubled congregant requires first an understanding of the nature of the problem. Once the presenting concern is understood, the PCP can decide whether she will be able to help the care receiver deal with the problem or if the congregant should be referred to another source of care. Oftentimes, a congregant's need is simply to have someone with whom she can share her circumstances—a friendly ear, a shoulder to cry on. In such cases, active listening is the PCP's tool of choice. Other times, there will be no solution to the problem, and again, the need is for nonjudgmental caring and support. An example of the latter might be the circumstances of a person who is terminally ill. She is receiving the appropriate palliative care and supportive social services but has no one with whom to share her fears, her concerns about dying, or her worries about how her family will carry on without her. Talking directly with a family member at this time may not seem an option for her, out of concern that she may unduly upset her loved one. Or she may realize that her need is simply to unburden—to talk about what is going on in her mind and heart without eliciting unwanted advice or attempts to fix things. In such a circumstance, the congregant's unfulfilled need is for a compassionate, attentive companion to journey with her through her final days. This is the role that volunteers for hospice fill, one that can be profoundly important to the care recipient (and sometimes life changing for the care provider). Meanwhile, in many if not most instances, nothing more complicated than compassionate presence and active listening are the transformative gifts a PCP can bring to a congregant.

There will be occasions, however, when a person will come to a PCP with needs that require action beyond supportive, active listening. Discovering what exactly the problem is that is being presented by the congregant and using that knowledge to help the care recipient identify the appropriate support or services she will require are the challenges of assessment. Here again, focused, active listening is the first component of an accurate assessment. Some congregants may be able to clearly state the issue that confronts them and what they need to resolve the situation, but often this is not the case. Indeed, care recipients, in unburdening, may begin a pastoral care encounter with information they need to share but that is not problem defining. It may not be until the very end of a visit that they are finally able to identify their problem. It is important that the PCP listen attentively to the whole story. In another common scenario, the congregant's presenting problem may obscure a deeper issue. In such cases, the PCP must be patient and allow the congregant's story to fully unfold.

As an example, let's look at the following case study. Jane makes an appointment to speak with Mary, one of her congregation's PCPs, and when they meet Jane looks harried, tired, and clearly upset. When Mary invites her to share her problem, Jane begins a tale of a working mother floundering amid the demands of raising her four children while her husband is mostly absent from their lives. Jane describes trying to get the kids off to school in the morning, making their breakfasts and lunches, getting two of the kids to the school bus, returning, and trying to keep the other two occupied while she dresses for work. She then must drop off the younger children at two day care centers miles apart and far from her office. By the time she reaches work she is exhausted, and the thought of reversing the whole process in the evening leaves her emotionally drained and unable focus on her work. The weekends are a blur of trying to care for the children by herself. After telling this part of her story, she seems calmer and becomes quiet. After a few moments, Mary asks Jane what occupies her husband's time. Jane replies that her husband spends evenings at work or going out with "the boys," comes home very late, and is then unable to get up in the morning in time to be of help. On weekends he is out of sorts, unpleasant to be around, and she feels it is better for the children to stay out of his way. She pauses again and then talks about trying to get help from her sister, who lives nearby, but her sister has young children of her own and is often not in a position to be of help. Jane pauses again as tears well up in her eyes. "My sister keeps asking me why I stay married to a drunk, and that doesn't help me a bit," she says, sobbing. Mary asks if Jane believes her husband drinks too much, and Jane nods yes and is then quiet again. Finally she says, "But he won't talk about it."

After listening to Jane for nearly an hour, Mary has learned of Jane's immediate issues—her inability to cope as a virtually single working mother of four young children. She has also learned what is likely to be at the root of the problem: Jane's husband's drinking. Mary's first task is to respond to Jane's immediate need: getting help managing the kids. Regarding this predicament, she asks Jane, "Can you tell me what would help you with your parenting needs?" She then explorers the possibility of getting support from other family members or friends. Finally, Mary asks, "How can I be of most help to you, Jane?" It is very likely that just being able to share her story will begin to give Jane hope that solutions can be found for her predicament. Responding to Mary's nonjudgmental concern, she may feel that she now has an ally in trying to solve her problems. Meanwhile, Mary can recommend resources in the community for families in crisis including Al-Anon meetings for family members of substance abusers, where Jane can find support, advice, and friendship. Mary may also recommend another of the church's lay ministry programs that can provide child care so that Jane can attend the Al-Anon meetings. Jane has identified her urgent needs. Addressing her husband's alcohol problem will not resolve her short-term, pressing need for help with their children. Mary is now challenged to be present, encouraging, and hopeful as she supports Jane's efforts to engage the resources she needs to manage on a daily basis.

If, after hearing her story, the PCP still finds the congregant's needs unclear, the PCP can ask the following:

1. Define as best you can what you need.
2. What have you tried already?
3. Describe your support system—family, friends, health care providers, etc.
4. How can I be of most help?

As the pastoral care encounter draws to a close, it is important to remember that the PCP is not obliged to have at her fingertips all the possible solutions to a care recipient's problems. The first step is to understand her problems and needs, and then be prepared to support her efforts to find solutions. One solution that is rarely called for is for the PCP to intervene herself; e.g., Mary should not volunteer to help Jane with her children. The PCP's role is to collaborate with the care recipient in finding appropriate solutions. Above all, a care recipient should be made to feel deeply secure in the knowledge that she will not be abandoned by the PCP.

In certain circumstances, a PCP's assessment of a congregant's needs can broaden in scope. Such becomes the case when a PCP is visiting someone confined to her home. The congregant may be recovering from an illness or a surgical procedure. More often, it will be infirm elderly congregants who will be candidates for regular pastoral home visits. When the congregant is rarely visited by others, the PCP should assess not only the congregant but her surroundings to determine whether the environment is safe and conducive to the member's well-being. The following checkpoints can be used to guide the PCP through such an assessment:

1. Consider the physical appearance of the congregant. Is she properly dressed and groomed? Is there any evidence that she is not able to maintain good personal hygiene?

2. Is the congregant safe and comfortable? Look for dangers such as obstacles to foot traffic, poor lighting, and hard-to-negotiate steps; also check for fire hazards

such as multiple electrical plugs in a single wall outlet. Is the temperature of the congregant's living quarters comfortable?

3. Is the congregant's environment workable given any disabilities (e.g., poor vision) or other special needs (e.g., maneuvering in a wheelchair)?

4. Is the congregant prepared for emergencies? Look for the accessibility of a telephone or preprogrammed medical alert devices.

5. Assess the orderliness and accessibility of medications. Ask the care recipient if she is able to organize her medications and follow the medication regime? Are there prescriptions that are overdue for refilling?

6. Check the kitchen for tidiness. Is there garbage that needs to be removed? Is there nutritious food in the cupboards and refrigerator?

In the process of reviewing the congregant's environment for possible hazards or other unhealthy signs, the PCP can also be on the lookout for objects or signs that may be useful in working with the congregant. Is there evidence of a hobby or special interest in the care recipient's home, something that might occasionally be the focus of a pastoral care visit? Similarly, is there evidence of religious or spiritual beliefs that could prompt a conversation about the congregant's faith? Generally, when in the care recipient's environment, the PCP should be vigilant for any signs or conditions, positive or negative, that could affect the well-being of the care receiver.

Understanding a congregant's existing support system is a critical component of any assessment. This includes learning about the quality of the care recipient's relationship to each member of her support network. If the care recipient is particularly close with one family member or friend, the PCP might ask permission to approach that person on behalf of the care recipient. Providing pastoral care to others teaches one over and over again how difficult it is for many people to ask for help. Reconnecting a congregant with her existing supports is often the key to setting the care recipient on a path toward healing and a new found well-being.

Collecting the information that is called for on the PCP's Initial Contact Sheet and the PCP's Contact Notes form (see appendices B and C for examples) should go a long way toward establishing a working assessment of the care recipient's problems and possible solutions. The Initial Contact Sheet captures such vital information as the care recipient's contact information, who referred her to pastoral care and for what reasons, the names and contact information for family members, neighbors, and other caregivers (doctors, social workers, medical equipment suppliers, etc.), and whom to contact in an emergency. Other relevant information or observations can also be recorded on the form.

The second form is the PCP's Contact Notes, or progress report. After initial contact has been established, it is used to record time, date, and other particulars of each pastoral care visit, facts and observations of the PCP prompted by the visit, and any recommendations or other reminders the PCP may wish to follow up on later. Over time, these Contact Notes form a picture of a living, caring relationship. They can be used retrospectively—to review the circumstances under which contact was made with the congregant and how she has benefited (or not benefited) from subsequent visits, what has worked and what hasn't worked in the PCP's care program, etc.—as well as prospectively: Given the pattern of care visits, it is often possible to anticipate needs of the care recipient, and meeting those needs can become routinized. As with the Initial Contact Sheet, completing this form also serves to support the discipline of pastoral care. In this respect, the Contact Notes become one of the primary tools for use by the PCP in supervision. This form is less detailed than the Initial Contact Sheet in its questions regarding the visit, prompting the PCP to use a more narrative form of note taking; the narrative can be seen as a chapter in the story of the relationship. And caregivers should not only focus on the care recipient but also pull back and observe themselves in the relationship. In point of fact, the narrative more usefully focuses on the caregiver–care receiver relationship than on either individual, since it is the quality of that relationship that forms the essence and focus of all activity on behalf of the care receiver. These contact information forms, once completed, are added to the care receiver's file.

Care receiver confidentiality should extend to the information gathered in these contact forms. The care recipient's file should be kept at church in a secure location that is accessible only to PCPs and the minister (PCPs may wish to keep copies of files pertaining to their care recipients, always mindful that the confidentiality of their content must be protected). That way, if the responsible PCP cannot be located, her filed information can be accessed in an emergency (see also section on record keeping in chapter 5).

Referrals

Pastoral care is a spiritual undertaking. It is about helping another find the strength to confront trying times in her life. The preeminent pastoral commitment is to share the struggle. The oath of the PCP is very simple: "I will not abandon you; you will not have to fight this fight alone." This promise of our presence, support, and attention can itself set the healing process in motion. Our continued presence lightens the other's load. Our expertise is focused on establishing and then maintaining this healing, supportive relationship and then, through reflection and supervision, working to improve our capacity for empathy, for active listening, for sensitivity to the spiritual in our encounters. It is in just these ways that we are different from other caregivers or service providers who have a particular, usually narrowly focused, specialty, e.g., a cardiologist, an estate planner, or a social worker. Our concern is the well-being of the whole person, in body, mind, and spirit, and so while we don't practice these specialties, we are observant for signs that one or another may be necessary. Indeed, we may be the agent that brings the care recipient into contact with the appropriate specialists. But our role in the life of our care receiver is unique in its breadth and depth. We are engaged by a troubled congregant instead of, or in addition to, someone with specialized skills that relate to our care recipient's life and health. We put this unique role at risk if we begin to act like a specialist, diagnosing a problem and recommending remedies. Even if, by dint of our professional careers, we have the secular expertise that might be needed by a congregant, being engaged as a pastoral care provider means leaving our professional role and expertise aside. But clearly, throughout our pastoral relationship with the congregant, we must be prepared to make a referral when a need for specialized care or service becomes evident.

Broadly put, we should be vigilant for a problem that could pose a serious threat to our care recipient's health or well-being. Signs that suggest a medical or mental health emergency should prompt an immediate referral. Another category of concern includes chronic problems that have persisted in negatively affecting a care recipient's life. Such a problem might be medical, legal, psychosocial, or familial in nature. An obvious example would be substance abuse, less obvious ones, insufficiency of income to buy nutritious food or pay for needed medications, or a lack of vocational skills to find meaningful work. Listed below are some of the signs that should prompt a PCP to consider a referral for a congregant. The rule of thumb for the PCP is that the provider of pastoral care does not diagnose or fix problems; the PCP supports the care recipient in identifying problems and then seeking the appropriate expertise to resolve them. Two caveats: First, do not make a referral hastily; it may take some time to identify the actual nature of a problem and avoid an inappropriate referral. Second, if the nature of the problem centers on the pastoral care relationship, the appropriate first step is to review the problem with one's pastoral care supervisor or in peer supervision. Problems with the pastoral care relationship are the PCP's, not the care recipient's.

If the care recipient shows signs of a medical emergency, such as heart attack, stroke, or other serious illness (dizziness, chest pains, or difficulty swallowing), the PCP should not hesitate to call 911. A referral should be considered for other, nonemergency signs or situations, e.g., if the care receiver is unable to perform any of the common activities of daily living (ADLs), such as bathing, dressing, or preparing meals; if a care receiver's living environment is unhealthy or dangerous; if the care receiver appears malnourished or if she is eligible for social services such as food stamps but is unable to avail herself of them.

In the legal domain, a referral should be considered if a care receiver needs help with an abusive spouse; divorce proceedings; an eviction notice; credit difficulties; preparation of a will, durable power of attorney, or health care proxy; or tax preparation.

In the interpersonal domain, a referral should be considered if the care receiver is having serious, ongoing problems with a spouse/partner, child, or in-laws; encountering difficulties with single parenthood or experiencing persistent grief issues. Any signs or symptoms of physical abuse should be reported immediately to the minister.

In the mental health domain, a referral should be considered if a care receiver evidences psychosis (delusions, hearing voices, hallucinations) or other behavior so inappropriate that it interferes with her ability to lead a normal life: displays significant memory loss, severe depression, or prolonged inability to sleep; discloses having been abused as a child, raped, or molested; shows signs of substance abuse, such as slurred speech, slow and uncoordinated physical movements, exaggerated mood, a charge of OUI (or DUI—operating or driving a vehicle under the influence of drugs or alcohol), or the odor of alcohol on the breath.

In the religious/spiritual domain, a referral should be considered if a care recipient suffers from prolonged guilt or shame or feels estranged from God, their higher power, or their faith tradition, causing them anguish.

The above list is meant to be suggestive, not exhaustive of the circumstances in which a referral by a PCP may be called for. But with any assessment there is one cardinal rule: When in doubt regarding the severity of a problem of the appropriate level of response, the PCP should not hesitate to contact the minister. As her experience grows, the PCP will have more confidence in her judgement regarding a care recipient's need for specialized care. The PCP may then wish to seek the advice of the minister to make the referral.

All of this information on assessment and referral notwithstanding, it must be emphasized in the strongest of terms that the PCP's role is not that of medical diagnostician, clinical psychologist, lawyer, financial adviser, funeral director, or professional relationship counselor. The skills and insights outlined above are meant to equip PCPs to be more competent, knowledgeable, and confident companions to their care receivers. Becoming overwhelmed by one's responsibility in providing pastoral care often follows on the well-intentioned but misplaced conviction that the well-trained PCP can accurately identify the particulars of a person's presenting problems and then fix them. The first inkling that one is getting in over one's head in dealing with a care recipient should prompt a consultation with the minister. Getting caught up in a care receiver's emotions, confusions, and despair is a sign that one's protective personal boundaries are weakening or have already been breached. Similarly, feelings of inadequacy and loss of effectiveness strongly suggest that one has moved beyond the constraints of the PCP's role. For all of these reasons, a PCP's close, ongoing partnership with the minister and a well-organized system of supervision for lay care providers must be dutifully and consistently maintained.

Ending a Pastoral Care Relationship

Just as important as the first pastoral encounter, the closure of a pastoral relationship should be handled with thoughtfulness and intention. It should be respectful of the strong bonds that are often formed in such relationships and should anticipate a sense of loss in *both* parties. The end of a pastoral relationship should not just happen, especially precipitously; it should be planned.

When do you know that it's time to end the relationship? The care recipient may initiate the idea, and if this is the case, the reasons should be explored. If the decision is due to the care recipient's observation that the relationship isn't meeting her needs, it may be possible to agree to work on improving the relationship before it is abandoned altogether. Such a circumstance usually will get a good airing in peer supervision. But more likely, the PCP will recognize that the problem that brought the congregant to her has found a resolution: The care recipient has reconnected with an estranged love one; a local social service agency has arranged for nutritious meals to be delivered to the congregant; a congregant rarely cries anymore, generally seems happy, and is functioning up to her full capacity; the care recipient has organized her end-of-life planning and feels comfortable now that her wishes will be met if she isn't able to make decisions for herself. If the PCP feels that the signals for termination are unclear, she can broach the subject with the care recipient. Regardless, the process should not be hurried. If the decision is made to find closure, several meetings can be planned in which PCP and congregant review the events of their relationship, what has been accomplished, and the healing and growth that have been experienced by the congregant. The PCP can bring into focus strategies learned that have nurtured the health and well-being of the care recipient. When such reminiscing feels complete, a final session should be planned marking a clear end point for the relationship.

As members of the same congregation, the PCP and congregant will undoubtedly see each other after their work together is done, and the PCP should make a point of changing hats—from care provider to friend and fellow congregant. Thus, the care recipient's resolved problems become a part of the past and no longer form the focus of any ongoing relationship with the care provider.

As mentioned above, it is worth emphasizing that the end of the relationship is often experienced as a loss by the PCP, and any such feelings should be expressed and worked through in supervision and personal reflection.

Assessment of a congregant's pastoral care needs is a talent that, like so many others, grows with experience. However, mastering the recommendations outlined above should provide one with the confidence to begin reaching out to others as a PCP. With time, the PCP will find it easier to trust the caring instincts that arise out of her concern for another. The insights of ongoing peer supervision and the mentoring and support of her pastor will also help to smooth many of the bumps on the new PCP's journey into service. Perhaps most important to remember in starting out is the simple but profound truth that the greatest gift we can offer others is our presence, a compassionate and nonjudgmental witness to their worth and dignity as human beings.

Chapter 5—Organization of the Pastoral Care Team

If your church is like most, you are already engaged in lay ministry activities, bringing care and support to needy members of the congregation. For instance, you may have a group, perhaps you call it "Helping Hands" or "Caring and Sharing," that brings food to those who have been incapacitated by illness or other traumatic life event. Perhaps the same group or another provides rides to shut-ins for doctors' appointments or for food shopping. Perhaps your church has a prayer shawl ministry providing warm hand-knit shawls to members who are going through difficult times, to let them know that they are held warmly in the hearts of the church community. By whatever name, if the activity involves members of the church providing attention, support, and services to other members, you are already doing lay ministry. So the first task of lay ministry organization is the inventorying of such existing activities.

The breadth and scope of your church's lay ministry will depend on the size of the church, its mission and needs, and its resources. Having just a "helping hands" group would constitute an important, basic program, and that group would function under its own leadership. For a couple of reasons, having several such groups providing different support and services to congregants would begin to suggest the usefulness of a central lay ministry organization. First and foremost, with a central coordinating group, information can be shared about members who might benefit from several church resources. Centralized organization would also help in the recruitment of new volunteers to the lay ministry, as well as in the coordination of ongoing training and peer support. And with solid organization, the always critically important effort to enhance the spiritual growth and fulfillment of the lay ministers themselves can be more easily maintained. While lay ministers understand that their work with a congregant is undertaken for the sake of that person and not to satisfy some personal need, it is in that selfless, altruistic activity that their own spiritual growth is fostered. Training and peer support can enhance lay ministers' growth as well as validate the importance of the work and the opportunities to improve their performance. We will have a lot more to say about training and supervision later. What is important at this juncture is that there are several good reasons to coordinate even a few lay ministry efforts through more thoughtful organization.

Since we are talking about church work, you can probably guess what our first organizational move will be: We'll form a committee! Each of the existing lay ministry programs should be represented on this lay ministry coordinating committee. Committee members would elect their own leader or facilitator, set term limits and leadership responsibilities, determine meeting schedules, and gather committee members' contact information, as well as create a mechanism for agenda setting (for instance, getting in touch with the committee chair before the next meeting to present an agenda item). There would not be much difference here from the workings of any other major church committee. The committee would be accountable to the minister, with whom it would negotiate the frequency of the minister's attendance at committee meetings.

Let us assume, then, that with an organized lay ministry in place, your congregation is ready to create a team of lay pastoral care providers. Members of this team will be assigned to bring comfort and support to specific congregants and their families in need of pastoral care. In the process, the PCPs will typically establish relationships that will include multiple encounters that may continue for months or years. (Individuals on the pastoral care team might also be assigned to a group of church members, such as the church's senior youth or to all the congregants in a particular nursing home, with similar expectations that they will make regular visits to their care receivers or be available to them as needed.) Such interactions are often congenial, low-key, and enjoyable, but they can also at times be difficult, tense, frustrating, even frightening for the care provider. So it is essential that the pastoral care team be well-organized and trained to respond appropriately to whatever may develop in the process of providing care; such contingencies also underline the importance of good self-care and recognizing how and when to make referrals to appropriate professional caregivers. Participation in all training events as well as supervisory meetings should · be required for all PCPs.

Even if the providers of pastoral care are experienced in social or health care services, their work in the church community will need to be carefully organized and supported, with close lines of communication maintained among PCPs, lay leaders, and the minister. A budget should be created to support their training and other activities. And it is important to emphasize here that no matter what a PCP's experience might be in the secular clinical world, pastoral care is unique in a number of significant ways. Indeed, it is because of some of these differences that people in crisis are drawn to a pastoral care provider in preference to, say, a social worker or psychologist. At the same time, such professionals are quite often happily surprised at how their pastoral care training deepens and enriches their traditional ways of working with people. So the training of lay pastoral care providers, even those with clinical or other service backgrounds, is important and invariably received with enthusiasm and gratefulness.

There are two strategies for building a pastoral care team: (1) congregants deemed appropriate may be handpicked by the minister, or (2) members may apply for the role of PCP (see appendix A for a sample application form), and their appropriateness decided upon by the minister. If the lay ministry committee includes some seasoned secular care providers, the minister may choose to share the responsibility for selecting the pastoral care team with the committee. But the parish minister is likely to be more familiar with the church's members than any committee member, allowing the selection process to be informed by a deeper knowledge of a congregant's character and suitability to the sensitive role of care provider. In addition, the minister's guidance through the selection process will give added credibility to those selected for the pastoral care team as well as to the decisions and choices made by the lay ministry committee going forward. However the pastoral team is gathered, its selection should be guided by the list of desired personal qualities of PCPs outlined in chapter 2.

When the pastoral care team has been gathered, they should be introduced to the congregation and their ministry consecrated at a Sunday morning worship service. Whatever form this service takes, it should involve the participation of the congregation (e.g., a laying-on of hands or a responsive call to ministry led by the minister). From this point forward, the minister should take every opportunity to hold up the work of the lay ministers generally and specifically that of the pastoral care providers and their availability to any church member in need.

The new PCP team should receive an introductory training and participate in regular monthly lay ministry meetings after that. If they don't already, these monthly meetings should incorporate a training element so that the skills, understanding, and rewards of lay ministry are regularly deepened. And with the establishment of the PCP team, each monthly meeting will need a formal supervision session led by the minister in which care providers can discuss their experiences and get support and advice from both the minister and their peers when needed. The training component of each meeting may be opened to any lay minister, but supervision can be restricted to those providing direct care to church members. The PCPs should also be represented on the lay ministry coordinating committee. In this context they can be kept abreast of congregants' needs as they are encountered through the other lay ministry programs, and the other lay ministers can make referrals to the pastoral care team where called for. Similarly, the PCPs can carry referrals to the other lay ministers for their services.

In a small church, all lay ministers meet monthly for group support, discussion, and ongoing training. A supervisory session can follow for PCPs. The lay ministry coordinating committee will be responsible for the meeting's agenda and running the meeting. The church's pastor should be in attendance at these meetings, and if supervision is scheduled directly after the general meeting, the minister will stay to lead that session. Over time, in a larger church with a variety of ongoing lay ministry initiatives each involving a number of volunteers, the separate groups may find it useful to have their own regular meetings and focused agendas. In one large church south of Boston, the "Helping Hands" group, led by three lay ministers, has a long list of ways they can be of help to church members, from providing rides to mowing lawns and moving furniture, not to mention the preparation of meals for those in stressful life situations. This latter function requires virtually constant activity by several members of the group. (Indeed, one member—"the Soup Lady"—who specializes in making and freezing large batches of chicken soup, has become "the Supervising Soup Lady" as more volunteer soup makers have been pressed into service to keep up with demand.) The "Helping Hands" team finds it essential to meet monthly to coordinate its various activities, including the ongoing solicitation of new volunteers. Meanwhile, the lay ministers who organize and supervise the group's activities attend the monthly lay ministry meetings, and one of them sits on the lay ministry coordinating committee. In some large churches, the coordinating committee may meet as frequently as weekly to review the needs of congregants and the effectiveness of their services to church members. Such frequent meetings, even though often brief, allow them to quickly take action regarding any emerging problems or congregant crisis.

Occasionally, all the lay ministers with their program volunteers can meet for cross-fertilization of ideas, brainstorming of new initiatives, and to acknowledge the accomplishments and contributions of all lay ministry workers. The lay ministers may also wish to plan occasional all-church events to bring the congregation together around a particular pastoral care concern or need, and the lay ministers should plan and lead a minimum of one worship service per year focusing on their work. Members of the lay ministry coordinating committee should represent the lay ministers in other church groups and activities, and speak for the lay ministers in church governance. The committee should also be responsible for creating and organizing the lay ministry training program and continue to maintain regular contact with the minister to discern how they can broaden and deepen their lay ministry.

The model of lay pastoral care presented here is meant to be applicable to any size church community. That said, the dynamics of a lay pastoral care program in a small church will not perfectly duplicate those of a large church. In many ways, including makeup of the pastoral care team and the focus of training and supervision, lay pastoral care may be more greatly influenced by a church's demographics—specifically, median age—than the number of church members. A church with an older membership is more likely to present opportunities for PCPs to establish one-on-one relationships with congregants that may last for years, e.g., until the care recipient leaves the church, a family member or other caregiver replaces the PCP, or the congregant dies. In a church with a younger membership, PCP interventions are more likely to be elicited by circumstances that are self-limiting, such as supporting a parishioner through a difficult divorce or the loss of a job. There is, however, another important difference in the dynamics of pastoral care in a small church versus a large one. In a small church where each parishioner has a relationship with virtually every other member, the interventions of PCPs will be more difficult if not impossible to keep private. Such familiarity among congregants may make it difficult for a parishioner to reach out to a fellow congregant for help. Such constraints may usually be seen to reflect a church culture that has not yet come to embrace the provision of pastoral care by lay people, and those constraints naturally relax as the culture changes. In this regard, it is important to remember that lay care provider programs have, among other goals, the modeling of how each member can be more receptive to the needs of fellow congregants and be motivated to reach out to those in need. The existence of a formal lay pastoral care program within a congregation should be a declaration to all parishioners that each of us can be looking out for the well-being of others, whether we are officially lay care providers or not. Indeed, we all know people in our congregations who always seem alert to the suffering of others and who are quick to respond, albeit in a way that brings no attention to themselves. A PCP program should call forth such empathic care and compassion from increasing numbers of the congregation. It is toward this end that the visibility of the care providers' mission should continually be a high priority for the parish minister.

It is not unlikely that a church undertaking the formation of a lay ministry will find itself creating its own organizational patterns in response to the demographics, specific congregational needs, resources, time pressures on the minister, and participants' work styles within the congregation. The important points that should not be lost in any approach to organization are the need for (1) maintaining strong lines of communication among care providers, minister, and congregation (the goal here can be thought of this way: Let no church member at any time for any reason fall off the radar screen of pastoral concern); (2) conducting ongoing training and supervision for PCPs; and (3) remaining vigilant for new ways to serve the pastoral needs of the congregation.

The Role of the Parish Minister

The parish minister's role in the lay pastoral care program will prove critical to the success and the meaningfulness of the PCPs' work and to the quality of care provided to parishioners. The efforts of the lay care providers do not remove or lessen the minister's responsibility for the spiritual well-being of all of her congregants. The lay care providers will typically increase the number of church members receiving pastoral attention as well as the scope of that attention, for instance, in providing a liaison to geographically separated family members of care receivers. But all the work of the PCPs should be understood to connect the parish minister to each parishioner receiving care. Meanwhile, the work of the PCPs ensures that pastors can focus their activities where they are most critically needed. There will always be parishioners whose pastoral care will remain in the hands of the pastor. It is also common for a PCP to discuss the need for a deeper involvement of the pastor in the pastoral care of a particular congregant for whom the PCP has taken primary responsibility (a need that may never have surfaced without the presence of the PCP in the parishioner's life). Meanwhile, a well-organized and supervised lay pastoral care program always significantly extends the reach of the parish minister, ensuring personal attention to more congregants than would ever be possible if pastoral care were left solely to the minister.

The principal duties of the church's minister in the lay pastoral care program include:

1. Selection or oversight of the selection of the voluntary lay care providers.

2. Training the PCPs. Once the program has been up and running long enough to produce some seasoned lay care providers, such folks may play an increasingly active role in training new PCPs, but the content and quality of training are the responsibility of the parish minister.

3. Supervision of the lay care providers. This supervision will take two forms: the leadership of routine, usually monthly, supervisory sessions with all PCPs, and the occasional consultation with individual PCPs who come up against an issue with a care recipient that they feel unprepared to address or in some other way

causes them to seek the minister's guidance. Often such consultations begin with a question such as "Am I doing the right thing when I...with my care recipient?" and the minister can help the PCP discern if a course correction is called for or, very often, simply provide the validation a PCP needs to get through a challenging time or experience with a care recipient. That the PCPs know they can always seek and receive this sort of support, advice, and validation for their work is critically important to the growth of their confidence as care providers and therefore to the quality of the care they provide. Meanwhile, the minister must be vigilant for signs that a PCP is becoming stressed in the care of a congregant and needs the counsel and support that only the minister can provide.

4. Connecting individual PCPs with appropriate congregants. In one midsize UU church, the parish minister assigns two PCPs to visit church members in nursing homes and other care facilities, and elderly shut-ins. The PCPs bring the church newsletter and Sunday bulletin with them on their visits and generally keep the church members abreast of church activities. The minister also assigns PCPs to individuals who need special attention but who do not require regular attention from the pastor. Importantly, when a PCP's help is sought directly by a congregant, that request is always shared with the minister. It must be clear to all church members that no congregant receives pastoral care from a lay care provider without the knowledge of the minister. In certain instances, the minister will also wish to make contact with the congregant. The

reality is that during difficult times in our lives, each of us can benefit from the attention and support of more than one person.

5. Raising the visibility of the work of the PCPs within the congregation. The minister should routinely and enthusiastically hold up to the congregation the contributions of the PCPs and their availability to all congregants. The mere presence of an active lay pastoral care program can be a great comfort and a point of pride for a congregation.

6. Promoting the activities of the pastoral care team as a model for how each congregant can be more attentive to the circumstances and needs of fellow congregants. There will always be parishioners who go out of their way to be of service to others but who do not choose to join the pastoral care team. The minister can also hold up the contributions of these folks to emphasize the spiritual values that are embodied in one's compassionate caring for another—at church, at home, at work or school, and in the casual, everyday encounters we have with others. The message is that all acts of loving-kindness represent our faith in action.

7. Representing the initiatives of the lay pastoral care team in the deliberations and planning of those involved with church governance and other lay leaders. This may include endorsing an allowance in the church's operating budget for the training and other activities of the PCPs. It may also include seeing to the involvement of the PCPs with special-interest groups and populations within the church, such as the youth and LGBT communities.

8. Monitoring the flow of encounters between PCPs and congregants to anticipate problems or to discern and correct any problematic behavior on the part of a PCP. Although the minister's oversight is usually accomplished in supervisory sessions, the minister must remain alert to the ongoing need of the PCPs for support and guidance. Ministerial oversight can be made immeasurably easier if the lay pastoral care team is diligent in its record keeping reflecting the particulars and the quality of each PCP's activities.

Clearly the parish minister will need to devote more time to the activities of the pastoral care team as the program is being established and settles into a comfortable routine. Once the program is up and running, the minister should feel an ever-increasing confidence that the pastoral care needs of every congregant are being met.

Initial Considerations for the Pastoral Care Team

At its inception, the special concerns of the pastoral care team should be focused on the following:

1. Communication

   a. How will congregants alert the PCPs to someone in need?

   b. How will the PCPs communicate with the congregation about the availability of their services and how they can be contacted? How will information about distressed congregants be passed on to the minister?

   c. How will communication among lay ministers work when a congregant receiving help from one lay ministry program seems to need other services (for instance, a lay minister bringing soup to an invalid learns that she would like to be in contact with a PCP)?

2. Record keeping

   a. The list of lay ministry services and service providers will need to be continually updated (such a list can either be provided to the congregation if the service providers are to be contacted directly, or maintained by the lay ministry coordinating committee after establishing a central contact point to receive requests for services).

   b. In order to capture when, if, and from whom a particular member receives pastoral care services, the coordinating committee should encourage the PCPs' use of the two contact forms described above. Not only will such record keeping be helpful when individual PCPs take vacations or leave the ministry, but patterns of congregants' needs can be discerned and future needs anticipated.

3. Training

   As we have seen, a well-constructed training program is essential for the education and support of the pastoral care team. But even if the lay ministers are not providing pastoral care, a face-to-face visit with a congregant provides opportunities to learn more about what might be helpful to that person. Any lay minister in contact with a member should be mindful of protocols involving confidentiality, proper comportment, etc. Since it is likely that a large percentage of congregants needing assistance will be elderly, the needs and challenges of the elderly should be subjects of special interest and education for all lay ministers. Regularly scheduled presentations by appropriate professionals will enhance all the lay ministers' capacity to help, as well as enhance their personal experience of their encounters.

4. Supervision

Any lay minister serving as a pastoral care provider may encounter situations for which she is unprepared or that in some other way make her uncomfortable or feel inadequate. The committee should discuss making arrangements for the parish minister to meet routinely with all the lay ministers or one-on-one as needs dictate. For the members of the pastoral care team, the need for supervision becomes a critical focus of lay ministry organization requiring more thoroughgoing and consistent attention.

Let us now look more closely at the first two of these concerns: communication and record keeping. Training and supervision are the subjects of the next chapter.

Communication

A perennial challenge of pastoral care programs, especially in larger churches, is the creation and maintenance of solid lines of communication (1) from church members to the PCPs, (2) among the members of the lay pastoral care team, and (3) between the parish minister and the lay care providers. In most churches, congregants are encouraged to approach pastoral care providers directly. Since one of the functions of a lay pastoral care ministry is to give congregants more opportunities to access pastoral care than can be provided by the minister, having the care providers directly accessible to members facilitates this goal. In addition, some churches encourage their PCPs to declare areas of personal interest and expertise, e.g., addictions, single parents, youth, end-of-life issues, and LGBT concerns, so that they can be contacted for this expertise. Designating a single care provider to take all lay pastoral care calls, perhaps rotating this responsibility within the team, may prove useful in some cases, as for instance when the minister is on vacation and the decision has been made to direct all pastoral care calls to a lay minister for triage. However, as a general operational arrangement, it is probably not as useful as the direct-contact plan. To this end, the pastoral care providers' contact information should be published in every issue of the church newsletter, on the church website, and, if possible, in the Sunday morning order of worship. This approach has the advantage of raising the PCPs' visibility in the church community and underscores the approachability of the individual care providers. Other strategies for promoting this group might include the creation of special "pastoral care provider" name tags to be worn on Sunday mornings or at other all-church gatherings. In addition, some churches use PCPs to perform selected functions during Sunday worship, such as reading the announcements or welcoming newcomers and offering to meet with them after the service to answer any questions they might have about the church. The point is that the more frequently congregants are reminded that they have a lay pastoral care program, the more likely they are to take advantage of it.

If there is no urgency, communication among the PCPs themselves regarding pastoral care issues is often best accomplished at the regular pastoral care team or lay ministry coordinating committee meetings. Clearly, any need on the part of a care provider for support or advice from the minister should result in a call to the minister as soon as is feasible.

Record Keeping

Keeping records of pastoral care providers' encounters with congregants, while not widely practiced in liberal religious faith communities, is considered an essential component in other denominations' lay ministry programs, and for good reason. A PCP's Initial Contact Sheet records information that may well become vital to the PCP or, indeed, to a congregant's family members and other caregivers. When completed, it forms the beginning of a confidential file on the care recipient, to which will be added notes from every subsequent visit. Over time, some of the information in the initial form may need updating, and indeed, every effort should be made to keep it up to date. The primary usefulness of the information captured on the form is to provide a source of medical and psychosocial data that will be available to caregivers should the care recipient become unable to communicate. It also serves as a resource for the PCP in contacting others in the care receiver's support network and can serve as a reminder of the all-important starting point of her relationship with the care receiver. If the PCP is unavailable or resigns from the lay ministry, a new PCP can quickly become familiar with the care recipient's circumstances and needs. And the record can be reviewed at any time by the minister. There is also a somewhat less practical but no less important reason for capturing and maintaining this information: It forms a component of the overarching discipline of providing pastoral care—a commitment to training, supervision, personal spiritual practice, supportive and affirming relationships within the pastoral care team, and self-care. PCPs who energetically embrace this discipline invariably become more invested in their work and derive greater satisfaction from its performance.

The care recipient's file may also be the repository of documents the care receiver wishes to have on file at the church, such as special requests for a memorial service, and directions as to the disposition of the person's remains after death. It is an unfortunate circumstance of life that many people arrive at their final days without having discussed with family members how they want their affairs managed, including their health care, when they are no longer able to do so themselves. These details can be recorded in such documents as advanced directives, also referred to as living wills, in which a congregant can itemize the medical interventions that she wishes to be used or not used when she herself is no longer able to make these decisions. Two other such documents include one that appoints a health care proxy to ensure that the congregant's end-of-life care wishes are followed, and one to appoint a person to assume power of attorney to manage one's financial and other non-medical obligations. Keeping copies of these papers in a care recipient's file makes them readily available should the originals become impossible to locate. Working with a care recipient to put such plans in place can be invaluable to both the care recipient and her loved ones. When a care receiver is no longer competent to manage her own medical and legal affairs, an understanding and acceptance of the congregant's wishes can markedly reduce potential confusion and conflict among family members, and decisions for the care recipient's wellbeing can be reached with consensus. (This end-of-life care planning need not be restricted to recipients of pastoral care. Indeed, mounting an effort to have all members of a congregation undertake such planning with their families can be a very worthy project for the church's lay pastoral care team.) As with any of the information contained in a congregant's file, these other documents should be revisited when appropriate, for instance, on the death of a spouse or partner who had been designated as health care proxy. Keeping each file current should be seen as a primary responsibility of each pastoral care provider.

Chapter 6—Training and Supervision

In the training component of any lay ministry program, volunteers learn the fundamental skills and behaviors that will equip them to be of service to their fellow parishioners in times of need. At the same time, they are guided and supported in building good interpersonal boundaries, confidence, and respect for their own thoughts and feelings as they minister to others. Attention to a well-constructed training program also expresses both the importance of the lay care provider's calling and the difference between this volunteer church work and any other. Training should reflect the deeply spiritual nature of the PCPs' interventions with their care recipients and the personal transformation that is possible through the spiritual gift of the lay ministry. The importance of the PCP's experience of her efforts should never take a backseat to skill building. Through training and supervision, pastoral care providers learn that their effectiveness in providing support and comfort grows proportionately to the deepening of their own spiritual center. When congregants seek PCPs in preference to secular counselors, advisers, or other professionals, it can be understood that the care receivers sense a spiritual dimension to their need—often a disconnect with their deepest values and beliefs, a disruption in loving relationships, or a separation from (or abandonment by) the mysterious, vital source of their life's energy and goodness, whether understood as a supreme being or simply as a power greater than themselves. If lay care providers are to be a healing tool at the disposal of their fellow parishioners in times of crisis, training and supervision should embody the strengthening and deepening of the PCPs' spiritual life. As we shall see, this focus on the PCPs' spiritual growth is rarely duplicated in the experience of volunteers in most other church activities.

Introductory Training

At least once a year, parishioners who are curious about the role of the PCP or are ready to take up this work can be invited to an open house, potluck supper, or other forum where they can share in the experiences, insights, and sense of personal growth of seasoned PCPs. (If your church doesn't already have a lay pastoral care ministry or any members who have had pastoral care experience in other congregations, the organizers of the forum should consider contacting the nearest congregation with an established PCP team and invite representatives of the team to attend and participate in this event.) At the end of the presentation, a sign-up sheet should be passed around to collect the names and contact information of people interested in attending an introductory training, with the assurance that participating in the training will not obligate them to become a PCP. This introductory training should be well publicized within the church and scheduled for a time closely following the open house.

The goal of the introductory training program is to provide participants with sufficient skills to begin responding to the pastoral care needs of parishioners. There should be no attempt to delve into all the nuances of pastoral care or deal with the many forms of crisis that can compel a congregant to seek help. Pastoral care training will be an ongoing enterprise, not only providing new knowledge but, just as important, responding to the real-world experiences of the care providers to make them more effective and comfortable in their work in the congregation.

The following is an overview of what may be seen as a typical introductory lay care provider training agenda. It is by no means the only possible scenario for such training and could be easily and productively adapted to the needs of one's church community and the resources at hand. The topical focuses, on the other hand, should be seen as constituting the most basic skills and behaviors necessary to begin providing pastoral care.

After an introductory chalice lighting and prayer or meditation, introductions can be made, followed perhaps by an icebreaking activity to help folks relax. The agenda and objectives of the training can then be reviewed. If there are experienced pastoral care providers present, they each can talk briefly about what drew them to lay ministry, recount some memorable experiences, and end with some words about how answering the call to this work has changed their lives. After these opening activities, attention can turn to what lay ministry entails and what it does not. And it is not too early at this point to begin emphasizing that it should never be expected to include any activity or anticipated circumstances that are beyond the comfort zone of the individual lay care provider. This aspect of self-care—the new PCPs should never feel that they are operating beyond their capacity to handle a situation—may relieve some unwarranted but not unexpected anxiousness in the attendees. It can be pointed out that even the most experienced care providers are likely to find themselves at one time or another in just such circumstances, and it is because of these eventualities that the introductory training program includes a component on how and when to make referrals to a more relevantly trained professional.

Along with a discussion reviewing the services that PCPs typically provide congregants, the attendees may be encouraged to imagine other lay pastoral care provider programs that might be outgrowths of the special needs or dynamics of their church. Thus, for instance, in a church with an active religious education program that includes youth members of the church's LGBT community, this might be seen as a special opportunity for the PCPs to consider ways to promote these youths' integration into the life of the larger community and to support and guide them in responding to any negative interactions they might experience in school, at work, or in other venues. Such a discussion would conclude the overview component of the training session and would be a good opportunity for opening up the meeting to questions, concerns, and comments.

Next, the group can be led through a review of the commitments that go along with participation in a pastoral care program, such as attendance at meetings, trainings, and supervision; record keeping of encounters with care recipients; and maintaining lines of communication with one another and the minister. In many pastoral care programs, experience has taught that limiting the span of service of the care provider—say, to two or three years, usually with the option of reenlisting—is useful for two reasons: First, it may make a PCP's commitment to the ministry feel more doable, and second, some turnover makes room for others in the congregation to step forward and join the pastoral care team. In small churches, this latter reason for term limits may be most compelling. It is also possible to devise roles for ex–PCPs, roles that require fewer commitments but allow for continuing ministerial contributions (for instance, as trainers or mentors) and participation in ongoing training and other aspects of the ministry that are spiritually enriching.

At this point in the training it is useful to introduce the subject of "ministerial presence." Beginning perhaps with a guided meditation focusing on participants' positive experiences with being ministered to, attendees can be led through a discussion of both positive and potentially negative aspects of how a minister presents herself in responding to a person in crisis. The positive qualities are then noted on a whiteboard or easel pad for reference throughout the training.

The following components of the introductory training focus on the single most important aspect of pastoral care —a skill that is used in every encounter: active listening. This can be explained and then demonstrated by the trainers—both good listening skills and those that are not helpful. The attendees can then role-play this fundamental element of pastoral care. Such role-play may unfold as follows: Participants separate into pairs. One person talks to the other person for two minutes, describing something important about herself, her life, or a current circumstance that is on her mind. (In practicing this skill, it is best not to relate serious personal issues.) The other person listens, interrupting only for clarification if she does not understand something that has been said. At the end of the two minutes, the listener recounts what she has heard the speaker say. The speaker then corrects any misunderstanding of her meaning and reiterates any important missing elements. The listener then repeats her understanding of what has been said. This process of clarification continues until the speaker is satisfied that the listener has understood her message. At this point, the positions are reversed, and the speaker becomes the listener, repeating the process. For the listeners to be able to recount accurately what the speakers have said, they must pay close attention and resist letting their mind wander. They should also listen without judgment and without preparing themselves to make a diagnosis or give advice. The listener's only job is to accurately and completely hear what the other is saying. Listening and being listened to in this way is not a typical experience for most people. After the role-play, participants might be asked first how being listened to in this way made them feel, and then how often in their lives they have felt really listened to. Sadly but invariably, many will find it hard to remember such an experience.

The importance of active listening should be emphasized and reemphasized throughout the training. Indeed, it is not an overstatement to observe that in many if not most lay pastoral care encounters, compassionate, nonjudgmental listening is the most important gift that can be offered to someone in distress. It may well be all the situation calls for from the PCP.

The discussion and activities around active listening may appropriately take up as much as 50 percent or more of the training. The spiritual importance and healing power of this technique cannot be overemphasized.

The next section of the training should provide an overview of assessment and referral; assessment of care recipients' problems, circumstances, and helping resources, and under what circumstances, how, and to whom referrals to a professional should be made.

The training session should end with a focus on self-care: how to listen and respond to one's emotions, thoughts, and reactions in the presence of a troubled person, as well as some general suggestions for creating or adapting personal spiritual practices that will enrich one's ministry. The training session can then be closed with a checkout and closing ceremony. It may be useful at this point to provide participants with a brief questionnaire assessing the perceived strengths and weaknesses of the training and capturing any lingering questions or concerns that the participants may have. These assessments can be used in the creation and presentation of the next training session, which will be the first of regular monthly sessions with more focused agendas.

The above outline reflects a program that can be delivered in one evening and the following day. All of the topics covered and many of the questions and concerns that might arise will become the subject of ongoing training, where they can be gone into in greater detail. For the monthly programs, which can usefully be scheduled for one-hour or one-and-a-half-hour time slots, the subject matter can be customized according to the trainers' assessment of the participants' growth in basic pastoral care skills, self-care, and spiritual grounding. However, a thorough understanding of the basic skills of pastoral care is the first order of business for these future sessions. These sessions can be enhanced and enlivened by the participation of invited guests, experts in the topic under discussion. The selection of experts can be based in part on their willingness to act as ongoing resources for the PCPs.

In chapters 3, 4, and 7, we look in depth at how a pastoral care team can respond to some of the most frequently encountered problems that will occur in the lives of congregants, such as grief and loss, end-of-life planning, depression and mental illness, and substance abuse, as well as the particular concerns of the elderly in our congregations. The bibliography contains many topical resources, as well as general guidelines for working with people in times of need. Some of the references, identified with an asterisk, can be considered a good starting place for a lay pastoral care ministry reference collection to be housed in the church.

Supervision

The word *supervision* has several connotations depending on context. In the business world it may conjure the often uncomfortable relationship between a worker and her immediate boss in the office hierarchy. In this context, one has to "answer to" one's boss, and any idea of mutuality or equal power in the relationship is usually absent. But the supervision of a pastoral care program is more like that encountered among providers in a clinical health care practice, where peers and the parish minister as supervisor convene to offer support to one another and to provide objective insight into a colleague's practice, particularly when a colleague has identified a difficulty. Thus, a particularly challenging case may be brought forward in supervision in the hopes that others in the group will provide new and constructive ideas on how it might be more effectively handled. Clinical psychologists in private practice often hire a colleague to provide them with such an opportunity for collegial insight when they find themselves on unsteady footing regarding one of their cases. It is this form of supervision that is a foundational component of any lay pastoral care program, one that we will now examine in terms of its facilitation, organization, and goals.

Supervision of a pastoral care team is facilitated by the church's minister. It may take the form of a small group ministry gathering, sharing some of the latter's most typical components and practices. Thus, supervisory groups are kept small (five to eight participants is ideal), and if there is more than one group, at the end of a designated period of time (usually six months) the groups can reconstitute themselves by changing the mix of PCPs in each. As a church's pastoral care program grows, the latter tactic becomes more useful and feasible.

The frequency of supervisory sessions can be determined by the PCPs and the minister, but they should never be less frequent than monthly. Finally, the confidentiality of what is said in supervision must be rigorously honored. With these guidelines in mind, let's look now at how a supervisory session is conducted.

Ministry is a spiritual not a clinical calling. For this reason it is appropriate to begin a supervisory meeting with the lighting of a candle or chalice followed by a silent prayer or meditation. Then each PCP should check in briefly (no more than three minutes each). The check-in may begin by identifying the care recipient, depending on that person's wishes vis-à-vis confidentiality, then should touch upon the following topics: First, what is the primary reason the care recipient is being visited? (Put another way that emphasizes the importance of the PCP-caregiver relationship, what is the care recipient looking for in her visits with the PCP?) Second, what are the PCP's goals for the pastoral care relationship? Here the focus should be on near-term goals or expectations, not ultimate ones. Pastoral care is about fostering a relationship that often becomes more encompassing than the problem that first brought the PCP and congregant together. So the answer to this question is really a snapshot of an ongoing process. Thus, the focus should be on how it is going now, both from the PCP's perspective and from the perspective of the care recipient as indicated by her thoughts and feelings. And finally, is there any specific issue regarding the relationship on which the PCP would like the input of the supervisory group? The PCP might ask for a very specific answer from her supervisor and peers, such as: "Perhaps you might tell her…," or a more general one: "Might you try a different approach to this issue…?" This last gets at the heart of the supervisory process: bringing the group's insights to bear on any barriers to a PCP's attempts at nurturing a healing and compassionate relationship. The formation of this question—"Here's what I need from the group…"—should be given careful consideration by the PCP prior to the supervisory meeting. And indeed, one's check-in should be carefully prepared in advance to get the most out of the meeting.

After everyone has checked in, one participant, chosen at the previous session, will be asked to present an in-depth evaluation of a pastoral care relationship. If another of the participants feels that she has a very serious problem or an emergency that she needs to discuss (for instance, a care recipient has talked about suicide, indicates a desire to end the pastoral care relationship now, is clearly being harmed by the misuse of prescription medications or alcohol, or is otherwise engaging in dangerous activities), that PCP's emergency would take precedence for discussion. Otherwise, the PCP whose turn it is to present an in-depth report would now do so.

There are several ways that in-depth presentations can be organized. The first, and perhaps least useful for the PCPs, would simply require them to go through their check-in again, adding more depth to each topic. Unfortunately, without organizing their reports around a more structured series of considerations, they risk missing the sort of pointed self-examination that leads to a richer reflection on the strengths and weaknesses of their relationship and the specifics of any problem they may be having.

The second strategy, designed to provide this greater depth and insight, has the PCP prepare for the presentation with a specific list of questions such as the following: What was the nature of my pastoral care relationship in the beginning and how has it changed? Notice that the question focuses on the relationship, not on any specific changes in the behavior of the care recipient or the thoughts and feelings of the PCP. It is useful in this respect to think of the relationship as having its own character and integrity, larger, if you will, than the sum of its parts (i.e., the two people involved). This focus on the all-important relationship and its dynamics is the ideal place to start in one's in-depth presentation. At this point the PCP may choose to supply some details regarding the mechanics of the encounters — frequency of visits (any changes here?), different venues, increasingly more phone contacts, etc. It can also be useful to mention any other caregivers that have become regular contributors to the relationship under discussion, such as family members, the church's minister, or a doctor or other professional caregiver, and how they have affected the relationship.

Next, the aspect of the relationship that seems most problematic and how the PCP has been responding to it should be discussed. At this point, the caregiver should share her immediate objectives for the relationship, including any problematic aspects. This subject can naturally lead into a review of how the PCP is dealing with any concerns she may be having. The PCP may wish to discuss her feelings about the relationship and the direction it seems to be heading in. In so doing, the PCP should pay close attention both to what aspects of her approach have been working well and what efforts have seemed less productive. Finally, the PCP can project a best guess as to the future course of the relationship. This discussion should prompt any specific input the PCP would like from the supervisory group; e.g., is there something she has been missing that is evident to her peers? Should a professional be brought in at this point? And so forth. Here a question might be brought forth that could help focus the supervisory group's discussion. For instance:

1. What were the PCP's goals for her last contact with her care recipient?

2. What are her feelings when she goes to visit (or in another way make contact with) her care recipient?

3. Are the PCP's expectations for her pastoral care relationship realistic?

4. How has the relationship changed since the PCP first started making her visits?

5. Does the PCP find herself looking at long-range goals rather than focusing on the visit-by-visit process?

6. How is the PCP defining "progress" in the relationship, and does she feel that progress is being achieved?

7. Is the PCP trying to "fix" or "change" the care recipient?

8. Has the PCP changed over the course of the relationship, and if so, in what ways?

9. Is the PCP trying to meet her own needs in the relationship?

10. Are there aspects of the care recipient's lifestyle that bother the PCP? What are they? How do they make her feel?

11. Is the PCP able to be honest, compassionate, and respectful toward the care recipient?

12. As the PCP looks back over her visits, what has worked well? What hasn't?

13. How would the PCP rate her own listening skills in the pastoral care relationship?

14. Is the PCP able to be empathic with her care recipient; i.e., can she put herself in the other's world and see things through her eyes? If not, what may be hindering this ability?

15. Does the PCP see an end coming to the relationship, and if so, what are the signs?

16. How will she handle the process of ending the relationship?

17. What are the most challenging aspects of the PCP's ministry? The most rewarding? The most frustrating?

18. Has her understanding of what her care receiver needs in the pastoral care relationship changed over time?

These are just some of the sorts of questions that can help focus a supervisory discussion. Such questions can be suggested by the presenter, by a member of the group, or by the facilitator. One such question might also be assigned by the facilitator as a focus for the next supervisory group meeting, perhaps prompted by a commonality of concerns or observations among the members of the group. Such questions may also be helpful for group members in organizing their thinking when it is time for them to give their feedback to the presenter.

Although an uncommonly used tool in lay pastoral care programs, another strategy for in-depth presentations would be the use of the verbatim (see example in appendix D), the mainstay of supervision in the clinical pastoral education of seminarians. After a pastoral visit, the minister records, word for word, the contents of the encounter as best she can remember. At the same time, she describes her feelings and her care recipient's behavior precipitated by the conversation that took place. If such a task seems like an impossibility—it certainly does to most seminarians when first presented to them—it is really not as difficult as it sounds. But the task does become more difficult the longer one waits after the visit to tackle it. If one knows that it will be inconvenient to write the entire verbatim directly after the visit, it makes sense to jot down some notes that one can refer to later. And clearly, one will never remember every word spoken during the visit. But the PCP will be surprised at how much detail can be recalled. Knowing that one will be writing a verbatim undoubtedly helps bring focus to the pastoral call. But as onerous or scary as the verbatim may sound, it can be a powerful tool for self-insight and personal growth in ministry. The power of the verbatim as a spiritual discipline grows in proportion not to how exactly one can remember the words spoken, but to how closely the emotions and the thoughts behind the words are observed and recorded. Verbatims are especially useful in the development of one's self-observational skills: How did what my care recipient say make me feel, and how did that feeling prompt my response? Was my response appropriate? Self-serving or defensive? Empathic? If it was defensive, what was the hot button my care recipient pushed? It is responsive feelings and behaviors such as these—on the part of both the PCP and the care receiver—that can become the grist for supervisory discussions. If one is honest, a verbatim invariably discloses vulnerabilities that are the leading edge of one's growth as a person and a lay care provider. Making supervision a safe place to reveal these sometimes difficult and embarrassing inner thoughts is an especially important requirement for having a successful supervisory group experience.

During the in-depth presentation, the supervisory group should exercise its best listening skills, interrupting only to clarify a point. Members of the group may wish to jot a few notes for the general discussion so that they can quickly bring their attention back to the presentation rather than letting their thoughts run to what they will say during the feedback. The facilitator should maintain awareness of the time: A rule of thumb would be that an in-depth presentation should last around fifteen minutes. With extenuating circumstances and at the discretion of the facilitator, a presentation might go a bit longer, but a fifteen-minute presentation should give the presenter a workable time frame for organizing her report.

When the designated PCP has given her in-depth report, it is time for the group to provide feedback. Feedback should always begin with individuals in the group expressing their support for the pastoral care work of the presenter and affirming her ministry. They may wish to call attention to specific areas where the presenter has shown positive and effective pastoral care skills or behaviors. Meanwhile, they should focus on the pastoral care relationship under discussion rather than on either the caregiver or the receiver. They can also address any self-perceptions the PCP may have disclosed about her ministry. Another focus may be the caregiver's sense of the care recipient's perceived experience of the pastoral care relationship. And if the presenter has suggested an organizing question (such as one of those listed above), the group should thoughtfully respond. In general, it is not the group's responsibility to volunteer criticisms or suggestions for corrections in response to the presenter's report. Far more valuable will be their affirmation of the strengths of the PCP's ministry and supportive collaboration with the presenter when she has solicited the group's thoughts on a particular problem or concern. The facilitator should watch the feedback process closely and be prepared to steer it back to a more neutral ground if it begins to turn negative. The facilitator may also hear something in either the presentation or the feedback for which she would recommend that the presenter consider seeking the minister's counsel and advice after the supervisory session. Meanwhile, the general tenor of the feedback portion of the meeting should be positive and supportive. It should also be remembered (the facilitator may need to remind the group) that the focus of the meeting is on the PCP's most recent pastoral encounter, not the entire history of the relationship, unless for some reason the PCP feels that subject is one on which she needs the group's input.

If the presentation and feedback are kept to approximately half an hour, there will be time for further discussion. For this purpose, the facilitator might choose to have a general discussion on one of the presenter's points or propose a related question for discussion.

The meeting should end with a call by the facilitator for any brief comments, questions, or concerns about the session, a quick check on how the meeting was experienced by each individual, and an affirmation by the facilitator of the ministry of the presenter. The facilitator then should choose one of the group to present at the next meeting. Finally, the group should join in a closing ritual. A couple of points are worth reiterating here: A supervisory meeting as laid out above should be accommodated in one and a half hours without rushing, and everything said at the meeting is confidential. Remember also that care recipients' names should be used only with their permission. In supervision, all members of the group should see themselves as PCPs to one another, bringing to bear (i.e., practicing!) their best pastoral care skills and behaviors. With this approach, the supervision session will become a highly valued component of the caregivers' ministry and deepen their sense of their sacred calling.

Chapter 7—Crisis and Opportunity

None of us can expect to go through life without encountering episodes of deep personal difficulties—emergencies of one sort or another, death of a spouse, natural disasters, forces that seem to come out of nowhere to turn our world upside down. Unfortunately, it is the nature of these shocks that, for the most part, they do not send warning signals. Since they are unanticipated, they cannot be prepared for. In certain cases we will describe such an event as a crisis. But while there may be some variations in our definition of the word, a crisis always displays several characteristics that are not shared by other traumatic life experiences. For instance, an emergency may indeed lead to a crisis in one's life, but it may not. As devastating as it might be, it plays itself out and we move on. For an emergency to become a crisis, we must respond to it in a uniquely personal, negative way. Thus, *crisis* always describes our internal, emotional experience of an event. Whatever the circumstances, we define it as a crisis; someone else may experience the same circumstances in a totally different light. So our first defining characteristic of crisis is that its reality is an internal experience of an external event. But what makes one person's troubling experience another's crisis?

Let's break down the internal sequence of steps that takes us from an initial low-level emotional response to an event all the way to the terrifying feelings of a full-blown crisis. In step one, a problematic situation arises that creates some tension in us as it calls upon our standard array of problem-solving and coping skills.

But in this particular circumstance, our tried-and-true problem-solving responses don't seem to be working, and our anxiety mounts. In step two, we keep trying the same tools. As their ineffectiveness becomes apparent to us, we began to become confused, and our groping for responses to the problem becomes less and less rational and organized. At step three, we might try to redefine the problem to fit the skills we possess, but still nothing works, and now we begin to experience the growing paralysis of being in crisis mode—nothing we can do seems to resolve the problem. We are helpless, and without outside help we will gradually become hopeless. This ineffectiveness of our old coping skills and problem-solving strategies in the face of a deeply challenging situation is the second defining characteristic of a crisis. We will overcome this obstacle when we discover within ourselves or learn new coping skills, new problem-solving techniques that will work in the present circumstances and in others like it. If we can grow by adding new psychological survival skills, our growth will become manifest on the other side of the crisis. Meanwhile, there certainly doesn't feel like any reason for optimism when we are at step three and in the grips of the seemingly insurmountable feelings of ineffectiveness, fear, and failure.

To psychologists, crisis is the outward manifestation of our inability to get our basic needs met, such needs as self-confidence, friendship and intimacy, safety, happiness, financial stability, and good health. The coping skills that allowed us to comfortably manage these needs in the past fall short in the face of the new challenge. And in navigating the life transition required by the crisis, we always encounter loss or the threat of loss of the objects of these needs, the third defining characteristic of crisis. Sometimes it is as simple as the loss of our sense of being able to cope with problems or of our old sense of safety and security in the world. But it might be the threat of losing the love of the person we hold most dear to us or of the source of our worth and identity as individuals. The threat of this latter loss is inherent in any crisis involving an unexpected job termination, especially after long tenure, considerable investment in being a top-notch performer in that position, and the confusing of our inherent value with our career success.

To get a better sense of how the experience of inadequate coping skills can escalate into a crisis situation laden with fear and helplessness, let's look at two crisis scenarios, each representing one of the two fundamental sources of a crisis experience: accident and psychological developmental change.

Susan—forty years old and divorced—is a vice president for international markets at a large New York bank. Well-educated and deeply devoted to her career, she has chosen to forgo having children in order to ensure her ability to perform at peak capacity and keep her career on an upward path. Over eighteen years with the same firm, she has made steady progress through the junior executive ranks and is poised to become one of the few women in the firm's senior management. Then, on a Friday morning just before the Christmas holidays, she is informed that she is being terminated and that she must clear out of her office immediately and will be escorted from the premises at the end of the day. Susan is understandably stunned. There has been no hint of displeasure with her work, and although the bank has undergone several rounds of layoffs, no one of her seniority has been affected. She arrives home that Friday afternoon to find the dress she purchased for the office party that evening hanging on a chair in the foyer of her apartment.

Susan is numb, overwhelmed by a jumble of emotions. From her perspective, her world has been shattered; she can make no sense of what has just happened to her. Over the course of the following days she finds herself holed up in her apartment, walking around in a fog, unable to tackle even the simplest of chores, let alone undertake any professional or social obligations. She is so ashamed of her circumstances that she finds it impossible to reach out to any of her friends for support or a sympathetic ear. She not only has no idea what to do next to get her life back in order, her deepening depression is accompanied by a spiritual and psychological exhaustion. We know what has happened to Susan in her work life, but what has happened to her psychologically and spiritually?

Susan is in shock. She has suffered the loss of her executive position at the bank, a job by which she has defined herself, and with it her self-esteem. She has never entertained the possibility of losing her job; indeed, she has never lost a job, and so she has no coherent way of even thinking about her circumstances. Dealing rationally with her firing is beyond her coping skills, and she is unlikely to get through this crisis without help from others. It is important to remember, meanwhile, that someone else in similar circumstances, while shocked and dismayed, even terrified by the loss of a job, might be able to start summoning strategies for understanding and assimilating the rejection and loss inherent in her firing, thus avoiding a descent into full-blown crisis. This point is an important one for the pastoral care provider to understand: No matter what the external circumstances, how any of us might respond will depend on how we are equipped internally—by education, experience, and basic personality development—to deal with the circumstances. Because a certain life event would not send *us* into a tailspin doesn't mean that the same event couldn't be an unmitigated disaster to someone else. Our first lesson here as care providers is not to judge the seriousness of a person's predicament by our own assessment of the threat level of the precipitating event. But before we look more closely at how we could be of help to Susan, let's look at another crisis scenario, one that was not brought about through an "accidental" event but by a quite normal and necessary psychological developmental transition.

Henrique is twenty-four years old, college educated, well rounded in terms of interests and hobbies, and well employed. He is outgoing and popular, with a large circle of friends. Recently, however, he has broken up with his girlfriend of many years, a young woman who his family and friends expected would become his life partner. After the breakup, Henrique tries a number of times to fix things with his girlfriend but to no avail, and with each failure, he becomes more frustrated and anxious, eventually resorting to threatening behavior to force his girlfriend to return to him. He finally gives up these overtures and becomes increasingly despondent. He lives with his parents and often now remains in his room for hours, quietly sobbing. His parents become more and more concerned and finally contact a pastoral care provider at their church. Henrique clearly needs help, but they do not believe he will reach out on his own initiative. The PCP promises to make the first move.

Henrique's crisis was triggered by a less obvious set of circumstances than that of Susan, but the similar, defining characteristics of crisis are clear. The story that emerges in his conversations with the PCP is that his girlfriend has become increasingly frustrated by their difficulty in finding opportunities and locations where they can be intimate. Since Henrique lives at home and she has several roommates, they have very little privacy, and repeated arguments have convinced Henrique's girlfriend that he is not prepared to move out of his parents' home and set up a living arrangement on his own. The girlfriend has made it clear that she thinks Henrique is overdue for such a move and that he is too old to be living at home, and this pronouncement disturbs him. Their arguments on this subject always leave Henrique feeling frustrated, inadequate, and directionless in his ambivalence about moving away from home. And it is precisely in that ambivalence that Henrique's crisis was born. Henrique has entered that stage of his psychological development when a person's need for independence begins to outweigh his need for the security of the family nest, a security that was necessary and appropriate during his younger and more vulnerable years. Henrique needs to be on his own, to fly from the nest, but his ties to his family and the security of their circle are holding him back. His ambivalence about going it on his own only becomes a crisis when the love for his girlfriend and their future together are endangered by his inability to make this important developmental transition. Our well-being in life always depends in large part on our ability to mature through such life-stage changes: puberty, young adulthood and independence, establishing a family and career, midlife crisis, retirement, and approaching death. As we successfully negotiate these transitions, we grow, building on earlier accomplishments and life skills but leaving the security of the earlier stage behind. These developmental transitions are always at minimum challenging and often quite scary, even traumatizing. But their successful completion is necessary if we are not to stagnate in a developmental stage that our normal psychological growth requires us to pass through.

Most basically, both Susan's and Henrique's crises reflect an inability to move forward, to learn from and grow past the crisis event. The other common element is loss—for Susan, loss of job and livelihood, loss of the sense of herself insofar as she has defined herself by her job and status, loss of self-esteem and self-respect, loss of self-efficacy, and, as she continues to decline into psychological disorganization, loss of hope. Henrique experiences the loss of his girlfriend and the threat of the loss of the security of his adolescent embeddedness in the family nest. And like Susan, he is experiencing the inability to get beyond this crisis situation, unable to seize upon any effective coping skills or problem-solving techniques. As their attempts to solve their crises prove unsuccessful, the threat level grows, as do anxiety, fear, frustration, and a sense of powerlessness. Ironically, while crisis is at best frightening and at worst psychologically immobilizing, it always bears with it the opportunity for a new level of personal growth. As mentioned earlier, on the other side of the crisis we will possess all our older coping skills plus an entire set of new ones, better preparing us for wider and deeper life experiences. That a crisis is almost invariably a path to a higher level of functioning may not be evident at the time, nor should it be the focus of attention for a PCP in the heat of the crisis. Yet the fact remains that for most of us, any real progress in our ability to negotiate the challenges of life almost always results from the turmoil, losses, doubt, and struggle of psychological and spiritual growth.

The invariable consequence of loss is grief: The emotional expression of loss is grieving that loss. Even the expectation of loss can begin the grieving process—a response called anticipatory grief. Virtually all significant change in a person's life, even healthy change, involves the loss of what was—a loved one or love object (e.g., home or pet), status or routine, a physical or an intellectual capability, a job, a cherished hope or expectation for the future. Meanwhile, the feelings brought on by loss may not be identified as grief by a care recipient. A grieving person may be frightened or confused by experiences such as erratic mood swings or crying at unexpected times, but once she understands and can acknowledge that these are often signs of the grieving process, it will be less difficult for her to accommodate these feelings.

In 1969, the sociologist Elisabeth Kübler-Ross presented a model of the emotional process people go through as they adjust to a significant loss. Kübler-Ross described the bereaved as moving through five stages of grief: denial of the loss; anger that this experience is happening; bargaining with a higher power to restore the loss; depression that may be brought on by a variety of thoughts, such as that life will never be the same again or that the bereaved is in some way to blame for the loss; and finally, acceptance of the loss and the feeling of being ready to launch into a new life. Kübler-Ross believed that everyone going through the grieving process would experience these same five stages in this order. We now know that a grieving individual may not experience these stages in precisely this order, that sometimes she might skip a stage, only to encounter it at a different point in her grieving, and that she may never experience one or another of the grieving stages. We have come to recognize that everybody grieves in her own way, on her own timetable: There should be no preset expectation that, for instance, in roughly one year the grieving process will conclude. We have also learned that regardless of this potential for a wide variety of emotional experiences that may accompany grieving, there is a simple series of tasks that need to be completed in order for the grieving process to move forward and to ensure that it takes a natural course and does not change into a more serious psychological problem—sometimes called complicated, or pathological, grieving. In such cases one's grief doesn't seem to resolve itself, and professional help from a psychologist or grief counselor is called for. As outlined by psychologist and expert on the grieving process Dr. William Worden, these tasks entail:

1. Embracing the reality of the loss. It is not unusual early in the grieving process for the bereaved person to express disbelief that the loss has taken place or is irrevocable.

2. Working through the pain of the grief. This task requires that the grieving person express her grief.

Indeed, it is resistance to this task that can lead to a problematic grief experience and the need for professional help.

3. Accepting and beginning to grow comfortable in a world without the lost object. This may mean a change in roles, environment, or social interactions, and it often requires the grieving person to redefine her self-worth absent the lost object.

4. Finding a new way to relate to the lost object. The bereaved must find a place in her emotional and spiritual life to place the lost object (memories and reminders) that allows the lost object's importance to be maintained but in such a way as not to interfere with the bereaved's ability to get on in life, make new connections, and perhaps replace the loss with a new object of affection.

In all of these tasks, a PCP can make a critical contribution to the grieving person's trials in the reestablishment of emotional stability and well-being, and perhaps not surprisingly, the most important tool for the PCP in this regard is active listening. When others have wearied of hearing about a person's loss, the PCP can be compassionately present to share the bereaved's grief. A PCP can help the bereaved sort through her feelings, clarify those feelings, and accept them as necessary components of the healing process. A PCP can also help in the making of new connections to people and activities that are life affirming, and support and acknowledge the bereaved's progress in sorting through the jumble of concerns and challenges of her new life. The PCP can be attentive to and validate the grieving person's emotions and experiences. But perhaps the PCP's most important role is to stay the course through the grieving process, companioning the bereaved even as other friends move on with their lives. Our society seems to have developed a low tolerance for a person's grieving beyond a certain point of time after the loss. It is particularly in this regard that our church can become a healing environment in which no one is placing limits on the duration of a congregant's grieving.

All the above may seem most appropriate in the case of the death of a loved one, but the feelings of grief for many other losses can be equally traumatizing, and in some cases stigmatizing. The PCP's skills as a compassionate, nonjudgmental listener and dependable companion on the grieving person's journey to recovery represent the profound gifts that a lay care provider can bestow upon a fellow congregant.

Although some of a PCP's interactions with parishioners will not involve crisis, many will. It has been estimated that as many as 90 percent of calls from parishioners to a parish minister are prompted by a crisis situation. When a congregant in crisis reaches out to a PCP, the latter's first task is, as always, to be fully present to the congregant, to actively listen nonjudgmentally and compassionately to the congregant's words. In some cases, just the venting of the issue at hand seems to defuse the situation, and what felt like a crisis to the parishioner loses its edge, becoming more an unhappy or unfortunate event that is within the power of the parishioner to deal with. This deflation of the presenting problem does not mean that the congregant wasn't experiencing a crisis. It does attest to the power of a sympathetic, supportive listener to allow the tension of the moment to dissipate and for effective action to more readily become apparent.

When simply being present to someone in crisis does not quickly bring a measure of calm and control, the PCP's next task is to make clear to the person reaching out to her that she will be there as things evolve, that no matter what circumstances unfold, the parishioner will not have to face the future alone. Just this declaration of committed and supportive partnership may bring the first ray of hope to the troubled parishioner—someone believes in her, believes she can resolve the issue at hand and overcome the awful threats of the present circumstances. If someone else believes she can weather this crisis, perhaps she really can. As in all PCP encounters, it is the promise of ongoing compassionate presence that can start the healing process.

The PCP's next challenge is to help the congregant simplify the set of concerns she faces. As a person's upset escalates into a feeling of full-blown crisis, it is not unusual for her to extend the sense of threat and loss of control to areas of her life that are not connected to the crisis itself. Thus, for Susan, the center of her crisis is the loss of her job, not how her friends will interpret this fact or what it says about her vocational skills or abilities or what life will be like now that she will never again, she believes, attain the sort of success that she enjoyed in her lost position at the bank. Crises also often arise as "the final straw" in a stream of untoward events, any one of which would have been surmountable but the accumulation of which has worn away any remaining energy for coping or problem solving. In either case, the parishioner may identify a litany of seemingly impossible circumstances in her life, and the PCP's task is to help unclutter the territory and focus on the central issue. As the PCP helps the congregant reduce the problem set to a more manageable size, the parishioner can begin to establish sensible priorities for action steps. Once the critical issue is identified, the PCP can encourage the congregant to broaden her perspective to include new problem-solving strategies. At the same time, the PCP can encourage the congregant to dismiss strategies that haven't been working in order to clear the way for new approaches. Meanwhile, the PCP's presence, calmness, and hopefulness will provide the congregant with some stability so that she can begin to regain her balance. The idea that answers will come, that the challenge can successfully be met and the necessary transition negotiated, will begin to seem plausible to the congregant as the PCP's message that together they will weather the storm begins to sink in.

At the outset of a collaboration with a congregant, there are two circumstances that require the PCP to consider a different initial approach. In some cases, a circumstance will present itself that does not reflect the focus of the crisis but must nevertheless be addressed first. Such priorities often involve matters of health and safety. For instance, a PCP receives a call from a congregant who can no longer cope with the constant drunken outbursts of her husband, outbursts that are always verbally abusive and sometimes physically so. She calls on this particular occasion because she is fearful that her husband will turn on their children, who have begun trying to stand up for her and protect her from their father. This congregant's crisis certainly focuses on the need to establish a functional, nonthreatening environment for herself and her children. She and her kids may need counseling. Her husband, if he wants to keep his family together, will* require help with his substance abuse, and when that is under way, the couple, if committed to making a go of it as a family, will undoubtedly need couples therapy. But the truly critical issue reflected in this phone call is the need for the caller to immediately remove herself and her children from harm's way. So the PCP's job may involve calling 911 to have the husband restrained from causing any harm, or, if he is not taken away, to help the mother find a place for her and her children to stay that night. The time to work on the family's central issues will follow the securing of their safety.

The other crisis circumstance that will require a different response from a PCP is one in which there is an obvious and immediate need for the intervention of someone with special expertise. Someone who calls because she is confused by symptoms that could be caused by indigestion or a heart attack should be immediately directed to emergency medical services. A call from a person who is clearly delusional or is threatening to harm herself or others requires the PCP to bring emergency first responders, e.g., the police, a mental health crisis team, or other mental health specialist, into the situation immediately. This need for special expertise may not be apparent at the first crisis call but becomes evident with more conversation, and the PCP needs to be listening for such an underlying theme and act upon it quickly when it becomes apparent. Meanwhile, this does not mean that the PCP needs to withdraw from involvement with such a congregant. Indeed, the PCP's unique pastoral skills and compassionate caring may prove to be vital components of the helping modalities that are brought to bear on the parishioner's crisis. In such circumstances, a PCP should seek advice and support from the parish minister, who can help the caregiver discern the need for other interventions and, just as important, the PCP's own role in the unfolding situation.

Active listening, reassuring the congregant of one's intention to stay by her side through the crisis, offering calming and reassuring words, and then helping the congregant separate out the central issue of the crisis, all these are typical components of a PCP's early contacts with a parishioner in crisis. Another is to support the parishioner in determining what action might most profitably be taken first. Even when there isn't a pressing health or safety issue, the care receiver may be helped to identify a first step forward that recommends itself not only because it may begin to defuse the crisis, but because, quite simply, it is doable—a small step that even in crisis mode the parishioner is capable of performing and that, even without the expectation of long-term benefit, may allow the congregant to feel a sense of personal accomplishment and effectiveness. Thus, Henrique, with the support and encouragement of his PCP, might consider calling his girlfriend to say that he loves her, that he doesn't know yet how he will resolve their issues but that he has sought help and is hopeful that the two of them can get past this obstacle and renew their relationship. If she will give him some time, he will do everything he can to work through the necessary transitions he needs to make. Such a call does not go directly to Henrique's developmental challenge, but it is a positive, mature, and hopeful statement of his intention to meet the challenge that confronts him. It is a baby step forward, but one that can give him a sense of efficacy. It is just such baby steps that establish healing paths out of the darkness.

It is hard to overestimate the healing potential of the commitment of the PCP to ride out the crisis storm with the distressed congregant. Especially in the case of elderly parishioners, shut-ins, or others who may have no family nearby, the PCP's proposal of a collaboration in dealing with the crisis means not only that someone else believes that they are worthy of concern and support, but that there is real hope that they can come through the crisis in one piece. After all, why would the PCP join forces with them if their case was hopeless! And it should never be forgotten that when a person reaches a point of desperation —hitting bottom, in the parlance of AA—the irreducible minimum requirement for survival and a return to well-being is hope. If it is only hope that a PCP can bring a parishioner who is at the end of her rope, the PCP has performed a service of inestimable value. For hope to emerge, the PCP simply needs to offer her presence to the parishioner as long as it is needed. Even with little pastoral care experience, a heart of compassion will prompt healing acts of loving-kindness. No amount of technical expertise or intellectual accomplishment can equal or replace a PCP's compassion, concern, and commitment to the care recipient. "God bless her; I don't even know exactly what she did, but if it wasn't for her I never would have made it!" Hearing such expressions of gratefulness, we who have been given the gift of providing pastoral care to others know exactly what that congregant means.

This chapter is entitled "Crisis and Opportunity," and several references have been made to the psychological growth that very often takes place in a crisis survivor. What we haven't said is that invariably psychological growth is accompanied by deepening spiritual values and meaning making. As a person expands in her capacity to handle the vicissitudes of life, the values that give her life meaning and purpose strengthen and deepen. Indeed, her crisis survival is a triumph of the spirit. Her new coping skills will be marshaled in the service of the meaning that informs her very existence. The ability to love will not be threatened by the loss of love objects. Rather, a loving empathy for others who have experienced such losses will grow. Particularly in the case of developmental crises and transitions, the arrival at a new stage of development can bring with it many uncertainties and unfamiliar experiences and situations—in general, an environment that can feel quite alien at first. And so the continued collaboration with a devoted PCP can be very important to the congregant. It can also be a real joy for the PCP to watch a care recipient work through her developmental transition and encounter the richness of her new world. The opportunities for growth beyond crisis include the opportunity for the bond between the PCP and the parishioner to take on new meaning. And while all crisis collaborations need not continue after the crisis is resolved, if by mutual assent they are maintained, there will be post-crisis opportunities for growth in the PCP as well. Either way, the PCP will have known the ever-deepening, ever-enriching gift of the call to pastoral care.

Appendix A

Application for the Lay Pastoral Care Ministry

Name _____ Address _____ Date _____

Phone (home/work/cell) _____ E-mail _____

1. What is your motivation for wanting to become a lay provider of pastoral care?

2. What gifts and experience (including professional) would you bring to the Lay Pastoral Care Ministry?

3. In what ways do you think you would personally benefit from your training and service as a Pastoral Care Provider?

4. Are you willing to make the time and service commitments involved in serving on the Pastoral Care Team? Yes ___ No ___

When you have filled out this application, please return it to the church office. _____ will contact you to arrange an interview.

.

Appendix B

Pastoral Care Provider's Initial Contact Sheet

1. Pastoral Care Provider _____ Date of Contact _____

2. Care Receiver
   Name _____ Address _____
   Phone (H) _____ (C) _____ E-mail _____
   Age ___ Gender (M/F) Marital Status _____
   Occupation _____ Place of Work _____
   Best ways/times to reach _____
   Church affiliation:
   Currently active? (Y/N)   Visitor? (Y/N)   Other _____

3. Person initiating referral _____

4. Others in contact with care receiver (family, doctor, therapist, close friend/neighbor):

   Name _____ Relationship to care receiver _____
       Contact information:
   Name _____ Relationship to care receiver _____
       Contact information:
   Name _____ Relationship to care receiver _____
       Contact information:

5. Circumstances prompting referral (include how long problem has existed, how serious, any other caregivers involved, etc.):

6. Person to contact in case of emergency:
   Name _____ Address _____
   Phone (H) _____ (C) _____ E-mail _____

7. Sheet completed by _____ Date _____

8. Additional information:

Appendix C

Pastoral Care Provider's Contact Notes

1. PCP _____ Care Receiver _____

2. Who was contacted (care receiver, doctor, family, etc.)? _____

3. Contact # _____ Date _____ Initiated by _____
    Type of contact (visit, phone, other) _____
    Length of contact _____

4. Notes and observations:

5. Recommendations:

Appendix D

Verbatim and Pastoral Visit Reflection

The following is adapted from a verbatim written by a chaplain in training after a visit with a hospital patient. The observations following the verbatim represent a reflection by the chaplain on her experience of the visit, how it affected her, her concerns in hindsight, etc. In PCP training such reflections can be a useful, occasional alternative to the more labor-intensive verbatim.

Verbatim

Patient's Primary Concern:
Barbara has just learned that she has a serious urinary tract infection (UTI) that will have to be treated before she can begin physical therapy for a repaired broken ankle. She has multiple health problems, and this UTI seems like the final straw to her. She is concerned about her now prolonged and indefinite period of recovery.

Plans:
Barbara's chart referred to her broken ankle, and although it listed her other health conditions, I was not expecting the patient's very depressed mood when I entered her room. I had made no special plans for the visit.

Observations:
When I enter her room, it is dark, with the curtain pulled between her and her roommate (and the windows on the other side of the room). Barbara is wrapped in a blanket

and reclining in a chair next to her bed. She looks both depressed and scared. I can vaguely make out some get-well cards taped to the wall, and there is a basket of flowers on her bedside table. I can see no other personal possessions.

The Visit:

C: Hi. I'm Stephanie and I'm from the chaplain's office. Just checking to see how they are treating you.

P: I'm OK. (She looks up only for a second, and very definitely doesn't sound OK.)

C: Have you been in the hospital very long?

P: Well, I've been here for a long time, since the beginning of December. Now I don't know when I'll be leaving. There is something wrong... (She points to a catheter.)

C: With your bladder?

P: Yes, with my urine. So they put in...

C: The catheter...

P: Yes, they put it in this morning. Watch it for two weeks, then see. I don't really care anymore. I just don't care. I was doing well, I thought. Now I've given up.

C: This has been a setback in your recovery?

P: I have all these "oses" — osteoporosis, osteoarthritis, stenosis. Then I broke my ankle...

C: Sounds like an awful lot to deal with. And then to find out you have a bladder problem...

P: I don't care anymore...

C: Do you have family nearby?

P: I have two sons. (She brightens up a bit.) They come in a lot. They're wonderful boys and they care a lot about me.

C: What are their names?

P: Erik. He just hurt his back. He's always had back trouble. He was just reaching for something—last week —and pulled it. Next day this basket of flowers came. He was in pain, so his wife finally took him to the hospital and now he is on pain pills. He has, you know, two ruptured disks. So he hasn't been in for a couple of days.

C: The flowers are beautiful.

P: They come in every day, or phone. The family doesn't want me to go back to my house. You know, I live there alone, for the past three years since my husband died. I used to rent out a room, but I don't anymore. They want me to move. But I won't hear of it. Now with this, they are on my back.

C: They care for you a lot and are worried about you being on your own.

P: Yes. (Long pause.) I always took care of people. My brother died in 1954. I nursed him. When my husband got sick I nursed him. Finally went to a nursing home. Three years he was sick...hospital here, hospital there. He dies in his own bed with me with him. I was always the one who looked after people.

C: Now you need to take care of yourself.

P: Well, I'm worried about Erik. His daughter comes and sees me. She works at Northeastern. She's really a wonderful girl—has a job in computers.

C: Do you have any other grandchildren?

P: I have four grandchildren. The youngest is a senior in high school.

C: Do your other grandchildren come in to see you?

P: Yes. Well, one lives in Brockton. She works at the big nursing home there. She's very busy...goes to work at 10 and doesn't get home until 8 or 8:30. She's a good girl.

She's been in to see me several times. And my daughter-in-law comes in to see me, which is really amazing, because, you know, it's not the same as being a blood relative. But she's a good girl.

C: Sounds like you have a wonderful big family that cares for you a lot. Maybe you'll have great-grandchildren soon.

P: Yes, if I live long enough. I want to. I would really love that. (She looks very tired, but less concerned than when I arrived.)

C: Well, perhaps I should go now and let you rest. May I come visit you again?

P: That would be nice.

C: Take care. And God bless you.

P: Thank you.

Reflection:

Barbara was not religious, but she clearly had spiritual needs that weren't being addressed. With the news of yet another health problem she had finally come to the end of her rope. What hope she may have had, just the day before, for her recovery from a broken ankle was now seemingly dashed by this newest setback and she had no more reserve. She seemed to be collapsing into herself under the weight of a heavy despair, and I believe she was in danger of sinking into a deep depression. It seemed to me she needed to rediscover hope in her situation by reconnecting to the love and concern around her—that she was loved and cared for, and that she wasn't in this alone. If she could reconnect to the love around her it might afford her some perspective on this new physical setback and give her the strength to persist.

Given Barbara's age and accumulated health issues, I would also expect that she is wondering about her ability to survive and thus she would probably be entertaining questions of her own mortality and therefore end-of-life issues and concerns.

When I entered her room she seemed already to have become depressed by the diagnosis of the bladder infection. I hoped I could draw her out a bit, turn her attention away, even if only briefly, from her latest setback, and connect with her to help her find some emotional and psychological perspective. I noticed after just a few minutes of conversation that she had a good sense of humor and could poke fun at herself, and I thought this was a good sign (and tool) for regaining her psychological balance.

I actually saw Barbara's social (familial) connections as her ally and her biggest potential source of strength. The cards and flowers around her bed said that she had loved ones who were in contact with her, and I felt this was an important positive. And even in her situational depression she was easy to approach and talk with, once she got going. So it seemed to me that she would probably not alienate the staff. (I have visited Barbara many times since this initial visit, and, indeed, she has become a favorite of the staff and of the several roommates she has had since she first came into the hospital.) Perhaps the most pressing concern I had over my many visits centered on how she would resolve her living arrangements once she finally did leave the hospital. It seemed unlikely to me that she would be able to be on her own again, or at least in the foreseeable future, yet she continued to assert her desire to live in her own house. This issue hasn't been resolved yet.

Another learning point for me was that I had checked her chart before I visited with her, and her admitting diagnosis of a broken ankle didn't seem that serious an issue, so I was surprised by her appearance and psychological state when I first saw her. (The staff had not yet recorded her urinary infection, although even if I had seen that too I would not have expected her to be depressed.) When she started talking about not wanting to go on any longer I was taken aback. I began to have those thoughts that run "Now what am I going to say that will make her feel better...how can I fix this?" But I fairly quickly just settled into being with her, being present for her, letting her begin to understand that I cared about her and the outcome of her health problems, family issues, living arrangements, etc. I learned a very big lesson about making assumptions from a person's chart about their psychological and spiritual health. In talking about this case in supervision, it became clear that for a person of her age and health history, a fall and broken ankle could be very serious, both spiritually and physically. All in all, I believe I was useful to her in helping her recall her closeness to her family and their obvious commitment to her, her health and happiness. I believe she also made a connection to me as someone who cares about her, and we have become friends over the months she has been in the hospital. She has had down days, but almost always I have been able to get to her sense of humor, and I think she has been the better for these visits.

Resources

* Highly recommended as a core resource for lay pastoral care providers

The Art of Listening
Burley-Allen, Madelyn. *Listening: The Forgotten Skill; A Self-Teaching Guide*. New York: John Wiley & Sons, 1995.

Diamond, Linda Eve. *Rule #1: Stop Talking! A Guide to Listening*. Silicon Valley, CA: Listeners Press, 2007.

Donoghue, Paul J., and Mary E. Siegel. *Are You Really Listening? Keys to Successful Communication*. Notre Dame, Indiana: Sorin Books, 2005.

Justes, Emma J. *Hearing Beyond the Words: How to Become a Listening Pastor*. Nashville: Abingdon Press, 2006.

Nichols, Michael P. *The Lost Art of Listening: How Learning to Listen Can Improve Relationships*. New York: Guilford Press, 2009.

Shafir, Rebecca Z. *The Zen of Listening: Mindful Communication in the Age of Distraction*. Wheaton, Ill.: Quest Books, 2003.

Death, Dying, and Loss
*Byock, Ira. *Dying Well: Peace and Possibilities at the End of Life*. New York: Riverhead Books, 1998.

Grollman, Earl. *Living When a Loved One Has Died*. Boston: Beacon Press, 1997.

_____. *Talking about Death: A Dialogue between Parent and Child*. Boston: Beacon Press, 2011.

Kübler-Ross, Elisabeth. *On Death and Dying*. New York: MacMillan Co., 1970.

*Levine, Stephen. *Healing into Life and Death*. New York: Anchor Books, 1987.

*_____. *Unattended Sorrow: Recovering from Loss and Reviving the Heart*. Emmaus, PA: Rodale, 2005.

*Levine, Stephen, and Ondrea Levine. *Who Dies? An Investigation of Conscious Living and Conscious Dying*. New York: Anchor Books, 1987.

Lewis, C. S. *A Grief Observed*. San Francisco: Harper, 2001.

Morgan, Ernest. *Dealing Creatively with Death: A Manual of Death Education and Simple Burial*. Hinesburg, VT: Upper Access Books, 2001.

Nuland, Sherman B. *How We Die: Reflections on Life's Final Chapter*. New York: Vintage Books, 1995.

Rinpoche, Sogyal. *The Tibetan Book of Living and Dying*. San Francisco: HarperCollins, 2002.

Human Psychological and Faith Development

Erikson, Erik H., and Joan M. Erikson. *The Life Cycle Completed*. Extended Version. New York: W.W. Norton & Co., 1998.

*Fowler, James W. *Stages of Faith: The Psychology of Human Development and the Quest for Meaning*. Cambridge: Harper & Row, 11.

*Frankl, Victor E. *Man's Search for Meaning*. Boston: Beacon Press, 2006.

*Gilligan, Carol. *In a Different Voice: Psychological Theory and Women's Development*. Cambridge: Harvard University Press, 1993.

Pastoral Care Theory and Practice
*Benson, Herbert. *The Relaxation Response.* New York: Avon Books, 1975

Brooks, James L. *The Unbroken Circle: A Toolkit for Congregations Around Illness, End of Life and Grief.* Durham, NC: Duke Institute on Care at the End of Life, 2009.

Capps, Donald. *Giving Counsel: A Minister's Guidebook*. St. Louis, MO: Chalice Press, 2001.

*Clinebell Jr., Howard J. *Basic Types of Pastoral Care and Counseling*. Nashville: Abdingdon Press, 1989.

*Dass, Ram, and Paul Gorman. *How Can I Help? Stories and Reflection on Service.* New York: Alfred A Knopf, 1993.

*Fowler, James W. *Faith Development and Pastoral Care.* Phila.: Fortress Press, 1987.

Howe, Leroy. *A Pastor in Every Pew: Equipping Laity for Pastoral Care.* Valley Forge, PA: Judson Press, 2000.

*Kabat-Zinn, Jon. *Full Catastrophe Living: Using the Wisdom of Your Body and Mind to Face Stress, Pain, and Illness.* New York: Delta, 2005.

*Kurtz, Ernest, and Katherine Ketcham. *The Spirituality of Imperfection: Storytelling and the Search for Meaning.* New York: Bantam Books, 2002.

Kushner, Harold S. *When Bad Things Happen to Good People.* New York: Anchor Books, 2004.

*May, Gerald G. *Addiction and Grace: Love and Spirituality in the Healing of Addictions.* New York: HarperCollins, 1991.

May, Rollo. *The Art of Counseling.* New York: Gardner Press, 1989.

Meacham, Denis G. *The Addiction Ministry Handbook: A Guide for Faith Communities.* Boston: Skinner House Books, 2004.

Miller, James E., with Susan Cutshall. *The Art of Being a Healing Presence: A Guide for Those in Caring Relationships.* Fort Wayne, Indiana: Willowgreen Publishing, 2001.

*Oates, Wayne Edward. *Pastoral Counseling.* Phila.: Westminster Press, 1974.

Patton, John. *Pastoral Care: An Essential Guide.* Nashville: Abingdon Press, 2005.

*Pruyser, Paul W. *The Minister as Diagnostician: Personal Problems in Pastoral Perspective.* Phila.: Westminster Press, 1976.

*Remen, Rachel Naomi. *Kitchen Table Wisdom: Stories That Heal.* New York: Riverhead Books, 2006.

Toole, Mary M. *Handbook for Chaplains: Comfort My People.* Ramsey, NJ: Paulist Press, 2006.

Weaver, Andrew J., Laura T. Flannelly, and John Preston. *Counseling Survivors of Traumatic Events: A Handbook for Pastors and Other Helping Professionals*. Nashville: Abingdon Press, 2003.

Wimberly, Edward P. *African American Pastoral Care*. Nashville: Abingdon Press, 2008.

Zurheide, Jeffry R. *When Faith Is Tested: Pastoral Responses to Suffering and Tragic Death*. Minneapolis: Augsburg Fortress, 1997.

Prayer
Aldredge-Clayton, Jann. *Seeking Wisdom: Inclusive Blessings and Prayers for Public Occasions*. Eugene, OR: Wipf & Stock, 2010.

*Phillips, Sarah Webb. *Pastoral Prayers for the Hospital Visit*. Nashville: Abingdon Press, 2006.

Steindl-Rast, Brother David. *Gratefulness, the Heart of Prayer: An Approach to Life in Fullness*. Ramsey, NJ: Paulist Press, 1984.

*Wikstrom, Erik Walker. *Simply Pray: A Modern Spiritual Practice to Deepen Your Life*. Boston: Skinner House Books, 2005.

Ulanov, Barry and Ann. *Primary Speech: A Psychology of Prayer*. Louisville, Kentucky: Westminster John Knox Press, 1982.

*Finally, the many publications and programs of the Stephen Ministries offer a unique and invaluable resource for building a viable and effective lay ministry.

In addition to the above, the pastoral care team should collect and routinely update contact information for community service, health, and legal organizations, and reputable individual service providers. These listings would include such groups as:

Social services agencies
Councils on aging and elder services
Adult day programs
Personal medical alarm companies
Home equipment and medical supply companies
Outpatient rehabilitation services
Medical and urgent care facilities
Alcoholics Anonymous, Al-Anon, etc.
Local transportation companies
Elder care and estate-planning attorneys
Hospices
National special interest groups, such as:
    American Heart Association
    American Cancer Association
    American Association of Retired People (AARP)
    National Institute on Aging
    National Wellness Institute
    American Psychological Association (APA)
Federal government offices, such as:
    U.S. Department of Health and Human Services (HHS)
    Substance Abuse and Mental Health Services Administration (SAMSA)
    U.S. Department of Housing and Urban Development (HUD)

About the Author

Denis Meacham was educated at Princeton (AB), Harvard (MPA), and Andover Newton Theological School (MA, DMin). He is a Unitarian Universalist minister, a pastoral psychotherapist, and a licensed drug and alcohol counselor, and has over 30 years experience with lay pastoral care programs. In addition to parish ministry, Meacham has served as a chaplain at several large teaching hospitals and hospice organizations. He is the author of *The Addiction Ministry Handbook* (Skinner House Books). He and his wife live in Brewster, Massachusetts.

CPSIA information can be obtained
at www.ICGtesting.com
Printed in the USA
FFOW03n1934110116
20330FF